LEADER'S GUIDE • REPRODUCIBLE PAGES

CONNECT

LIFE & CHRISTIAN FAITH FOR YOUNG TEENS

VOLUME 9

TABLE OF C·O·N·T

CONNECT

ENTS

CONNECT Life and Christian Faith for Young Teens Volume 9 (ISBN 0-687-72641-7)

Printed in the United States of America.

This publication is printed on recycled, acid-free paper.

EDITORIAL AND DESIGN TEAM
John P. Gilbert, *Editor*
Debra Ball-Kilbourne, *Editor*
Cindy L. Caldwell, *Production Editor*
Phillip D. Francis, *Design Supervisor*
J. S. Laughbaum, *Designer*

ADMINISTRATIVE TEAM
Neil M. Alexander, *Publisher*
Harriett Jane Olson, *Vice President*
Duane A. Ewers, *Executive Editor of Teaching and Study Resources*
M. Steven Games, *Senior Editor of Youth Publications*

Cover photography by Comstock.

98 99 00 01 02 03 04 05 06 07—10 9 8 7 6 5 4 3 2 1

Abingdon Press

WHAT IS CONNECT?

CONNECT OFFERS

- reproducible student pages
- a balance of short, lively units on Bible, life, and faith
- a 1-2-3 teaching plan with plenty of options
- activities that will appeal to various learning styles
- a session-at-a-glance chart
- last-minute, easy preparation options for substitute teachers
- bonus pages for parents, worship planners, broadly graded classes
- perforated pages

➤ HOW CAN WE BE A POSITIVE INFLUENCE IN THE LIFE OF YOUTH?

➤ HOW DO WE KEEP YOUTH INVOLVED IN THE LIFE OF THE CHURCH?

➤ HOW DO WE HELP THEM GROW IN FAITH?

CONNECT will help you deal with these concerns by connecting with younger adolescents at the level of their basic life issues and needs.

The connections are based on a combination of

1. the developmental needs of early adolescents
2. key elements in the Bible and Christian faith
3. tying Bible and faith to life

Part of the process of developing **CONNECT** was to give youth from all over the nation a list of topics and to ask:

- What are the questions you have about this topic?
- What are your issues?

We asked them to be blunt and honest and to push the edges. Our writers used these questions in developing the units and sessions. So you have material for dealing with real life concerns from real youth, not something dreamed up somewhere far removed.

WHAT'S IN A UNIT?

TITLE PAGE

shows the unit title and the session titles; offers a brief purpose statement and tough questions about that topic.

This Is Not Junk Mail!

may be duplicated and given to parents, guardians, and other interested adults so that they:

- know what the unit is about and know how they can encourage or participate in conversations about the topic at home.

- understand the importance of the topic for youth and understand tough questions or realities that youth face about the topic.
- discover ways to incorporate the topic into family activities.
- become more familiar with young adolescent developmental issues.

Hallelujah!

offers suggestions for worship in the class setting. Hallelujah! can be duplicated and given to the pastor, choir director, and members of the worship work area in your congregation. Folks can use the worship materials and ideas to help make worship more "youth friendly."

Miscellany

is designed to help teachers who have both middle schoolers and high school youth in the same class. Miscellany gives tips on how to use the unit material with a wide age range, suggestions for special activities and projects, or ideas for intergenerational activities.

Following these unit pages will be session plans for one to three sessions.

WHAT'S IN A SESSION PLAN?

Each session has a specific lesson plan, with options.

Read Me

includes Bible background, material on the teachings of the church, background on the issue or topic, statistical information, developmental background on younger adolescents, and questions youth have about the topic. Read the Read Me page(s) in preparation for every session.

also known as the YouthPage, may be duplicated and given to youth. In most sessions, this includes activities related to one or more of the options in the lesson plan.

There are five connections in each session.
They are:

Initial **CONNECTION**

CONNECT with the Session

CONNECT with the Bible and the Faith Community

CONNECT with Life

Closing **CONNECTION**

YOU ARE IMPORTANT

Younger adolescents need positive relationships with adults. Positive social interaction with adults and peers is extremely important to young adolescents, and you have an opportunity to play an important part in their lives. You will facilitate a group experience from which youth may establish friendships, self-identity, and faith. Youth need someone who will establish appropriate boundaries and allow them to discover who they are becoming, allow them to belong to a caring community, and allow them to explore and establish their beliefs.

That person is **YOU!**

WHO ARE MY YOUTH?

A major research project conducted for The United Methodist Publishing House showed that, in every class, there are basically three kinds of youth.

55% of the youth surveyed are most interested in

- ➤ faith and relationship to God;
- ➤ tying the Bible to today's issues;
- ➤ learning about the Bible.

30% of the youth surveyed are most interested in

- ➤ belonging;
- ➤ a safe place to ask tough questions;
- ➤ current events (personal);
- ➤ helping others;
- ➤ informal talk and music.

14% of the youth surveyed are interested in

- ➤ faith and relationship with God;
- ➤ current issues, such as the environment, racism, poverty.

One of the keys to involving the class is to offer a variety of activities, with some that appeal to each of these three groups.

HOW DO I SELECT ACTIVITIES FOR MY CLASS?

Each learning activity is designed to achieve a Desired Result. For each Desired Result, choose the option most suited to your class. Try to choose options that will appeal to the youth in your class. If you have more than 45 minutes, you may want to select additional options.

As you "customize" your session, be sure you consider activities that are active and experiential, as well as some that involve discussion and reflection. Be sure to open your class with an activity that gets the attention of the youth. This will help them be receptive to the remainder of the activities. Bringing your class session to an appropriate close is also important. The Closing Connection offers an activity for this. You may also want to use some suggestions from the Hallelujah! page to open or close each session.

S

IF YOU ARE A SUBSTITUTE, LOOK FOR THIS ICON *beside the learning activities in each session. These activities can be done with a minimum of preparation and traditional supplies.*

THE SEVEN DEVELOPMENTAL NEEDS OF YOUNG ADOLESCENTS
(HOW CONGREGATIONS CAN SUPPORT YOUTH)

Because of their enormous developmental diversity, ten to fifteen-year-olds require a variety of types and levels of activities designed to meet the seven needs listed below.

1. POSITIVE SOCIAL INTERACTION WITH ADULTS AND PEERS

Because of their changing relationships with adults, especially parents, and the increasing importance of peers, positive social interaction with these groups is extremely important to young adolescents. Churches can encourage peer interaction by offering small-group activities. Positive social interactions between adults and youth are facilitated by mentoring relationships, participation in activities, and informal contact outside the church.

2. STRUCTURE AND CLEAR LIMIT

Youth ministries that are responsive to the young adolescent's need for structure have clearly stated rules and expectations that are generally accepted and understood by youth and youth leaders. One way of assuring acceptance is to involve students in the establishment of rules and the consequences for failing to observe them. Young adolescents need the security provided by clear limits in order to learn and grow during a time of rapid and persuasive change. Youth ministries should avoid rigid structure and excessive limits because they invite dependency, hostility, withdrawal, and rebellion.

3. COMPETENCE AND ACHIEVEMENT

Congregations can meet these two needs by emphasizing active learning settings, positive expectations of all youth, generous (yet meaningful) praise, and numerous opportunities for increased independence and responsibility. A variety of teaching methods, high-interest learning times, and activities provide a diversity of rewards so that each student can be successful at something.

4. CREATIVE EXPRESSION

Opportunities to express creatively their new feelings, interests, abilities, and thoughts in church helps youth understand and accept the new people they are becoming. Learning times with high-interest exploratory activities such as drama, music, cooking, painting a mural, and making up games for younger children, are all avenues for satisfying this expression.

5. PHYSICAL ACTIVITY

Responsive churches provide structured outlets for the physical energy of young adolescents rather than ignoring or trying to suppress it. Noncompetitive physical activities can be an integral part of the opportunities offered by the church. Teachers and leaders also provide opportunities for students to move around in the classroom.

6. MEANINGFUL PARTICIPATION IN THEIR FAMILIES, SCHOOLS, COMMUNITIES

Youth initiated Bible study, committees, and community improvement projects such as designing and constructing recreation areas or learning resources, are only a few ways congregations can engage youth in these areas. Churches can also offer opportunities for youth to extend their new knowledge and competencies by contributing to their communities through service projects.

7. SELF-DEFINITION

Youth ministries can help youth integrate their developing capabilities, interests, and relations into a sense of who they are and their maturing faith. For example, a faith development project might include keeping a diary and writing weekly summaries. Missions emphasis could focus on adolescence in various countries and eras. Youth should be encouraged to pursue answers to their own questions as well as their leaders'. Learning times could focus on helping youth create personal meaning and understanding in faith development, career decisions, family relations, and sexuality.

Adapted from *The 7 Developmental Needs of Young Adolescents (How Schools Can Respond)*
The Search Institute
700 South 3rd Street
Suite 210
Minneapolis, MN 55415
1-800-888-3820
Used by permission.

MINI-WORKSHOP

THE MUSICAL WORLD OF THE ADOLESCENT
(OR HOW TO STAY SANE WHILE TEEN ANGST BLARES THROUGH BEDROOM WALLS!)
BY JIM NIEDERMAIER

CONNECT WITH THE PARTICIPANTS

SAY:

➤ **I would like to welcome you to this workshop on the role of music in the adolescent's life. Music has been a hotly debated subject for decades. Many strongly held opinions surround the subject. We are here today because we want to develop a better understanding of and a more positive relationship with our teens regarding their musical choices.**

A MUSIC QUIZ

SAY:

➤ **Let's take a few minutes to remember our own musical background. I'm going to read you the following musical history questions. Shout out the answer if you know.**

1. This group had its origin in skiffle music. They got their original name, "The Quarry Men," from the school that one of them attended: The Quarry Bank High School for Boys. **(ANSWER: The Beatles)**

2. This performer, born Jerry Jiles Richardson, nicknamed himself after his ample size. On February 2, 1959 he persuaded Waylon Jennings to give up his seat on a chartered plane. Early the next morning, the aircraft took off from Mason City Airport and within minutes crashed, killing Buddy Holly, Richie Valens, and this performer. **(ANSWER: The Big Bopper)**

3. This talented family duo experienced disaster when its younger member died at age 32 from "heartbeat irregularities brought on by chemical imbalances associated with anorexia nervosa." **(ANSWER: The Carpenters)**

4. This performer was a member of the Brooklyn Heights Choir. In 1971 he advertised for help to perform "story songs" that he had written. One of his best known songs, "Cats in the Cradle," is based on a poem by his wife about a neglectful father. **(ANSWER: Harry Chapin)**

5. This group's lead singer, known for his substantial abuse of alcohol, is buried in the Père Lachaise Cemetery in Paris with such notables as Oscar Wilde and Chopin. **(ANSWER: The Doors/Jim Morrison)**

6. This group's song, "Rock Around the Clock" marks the very first number-one song in rock and roll history. Many regard the song as the birth of rock and roll. **(ANSWER: Bill Haley and the Comets)**

7. In 1965 an audition of 437 hopefuls, including Charles Manson, was held for a new TV sitcom based on a Beatles-type group. The four chosen for the parts went on to star in a successful TV program that also began a monthly magazine and earned the group a star on the Hollywood Walk of Fame. **(ANSWER: The Monkees)**

8. Once hoped to be the female Bob Dylan, this singer and daughter of a co-founder of Simon and Schuster Publishing Company married James Taylor in 1972. **(ANSWER: Carly Simon)**

9. This group's founder, who auditioned unsuccessfully for the Monkees, later formed a rock group with a triple lead singer line-up. The name of the group was taken from an Australian outback expression used to describe an extremely cold night. **(ANSWER: Three Dog Night)**

10. This group, originally named The High Numbers, later changed their name to avoid sounding like an advertisement for a bingo session. The ceiling at their regular venue was so low that the guitar player's swinging style often brought down chunks of it. This earned them an abiding reputation for equipment destruction that remained for years. **(ANSWER: The WHO)**

B GET ACQUAINTED

Before the session, make copies of the "Let's Get Acquainted" worksheet on page 14. Hand the copies out to the participants and ask them to complete the worksheet.

SAY:

➤ **This worksheet contains twelve different situations or events. Find someone who fits each description and have him or her sign beside that description. Try to find as many different people as possible. The first person to fill his or her sheet with signatures wins.**

When the exercise is over, go over the situations on the worksheets, asking participants to indicate which descriptions they signed. Encourage participants to elaborate on their particular experiences.

CONNECT WITH OUR ADOLESCENCE

SAY:

➤ **Sometimes we forget the struggles we faced and the mistakes we made during our own adolescence. Let's transport ourselves back to our early teen years.**

Ahead of time, record a variety of songs, about 20 seconds of each (for example, a worship song, an "oldie," a heavy metal song, a love song, a pop dance tune). If this is not possible, bring the recordings with you to be played. Ask the participants to close their eyes and listen to the music. After the selections are played,

ASK:

➤ **Can you describe the feelings or memories that one or more of these songs evoked?**

➤ **Can you remember any of the circumstances surrounding the first time you heard this song?**

➤ **Did any of these songs cause you to feel relaxed? excited? tense?**

CONNECT WITH CONTEMPORARY ADOLESCENT LIFE

SAY:

➤ **Musical tastes and choices are as varied as fingerprints. Peer pressure, time, place, and circumstance all play a role in the music adolescents listen to. Understanding why another person chooses certain styles or groups may help you to better understand an individual. Here are some of the reasons why music is important to an adolescent.**

After reviewing the following motivations behind the kinds of music that teens listen to, hand out copies of the musical choices chart to each participant. Work through the chart, taking time to discuss each item as a group.

POPULARITY
This person is compelled to listen to the same music as everyone else in order to be "cool."

BELONGING
This person feels abandoned or rejected. He or she feels a sense of community with the music and with the other people who listen to it.

REBELLION
A number of causes can lead this person to express anger and hostility vicariously through his or her choice of music.

FANTASY
A lack of healthy self-image may cause this person to use music to fulfill his or her innermost dreams.

EXPRESSION
This person uses music to express inner thoughts or feelings.

IDENTITY
Groups or songs provide a character or basis for the type of person that a teen wants to be.

WORSHIP
Music leads this person into and through expressions of praise and thankfulness.

POWER
An actual or perceived weakness causes this person to use music as a source of strength to overcome his or her oppressors or oppression.

RELAXATION
This person uses music to create or sustain a desired mood.

DISTRACTION
This person uses music to drown out the cares or problems of the moment.

DEEPER CONNECTIONS

SAY:

➤ **Now that you've had a chance to investigate some of the reasons behind an adolescent's musical choices, try to match the labels on the left with the statements on the right.** (These are included on the handout on page 16.)

A. Popularity	1. It's the cool thing to listen to.
B. Identity	2. I become what I've dreamed of being.
C. Belonging	3. I can play it loud and block out everything.
D. Worship	4. It helps me "chill out."
E. Rebellion	5. I can praise God through song.
F. Power	6. It allows me to escape the adult world.
G. Fantasy	7. I use music to express myself.
H. Relaxation	8. It fills a void in my life.
I. Expression	9. When I listen, I feel that I can beat the bullies in my life.
J. Distraction	10. I confide in my music and I can relate to it.

Answer key: A—1; B—10; C—8; D—5; E—6; F—9; G—2; H—4; I—7; J—3.

CONNECT WITH THE COMMUNITY OF FAITH

TWELVE STEPS OF MUSIC TOLERANCE FOR PARENTS OF ADOLESCENTS

SAY:

➤ **There may be occasions when we feel compelled to intervene in a teen's musical choices. We may better influence our teen's choices through acceptance and understanding. Condemning a person's musical choices is often perceived as condemning the person as well. You will accomplish more with your teen by listening to her or him and showing an interest in the music that is important to your teen. Consider using this twelve-step approach.**

Hand out copies of the "Twelve Steps of Music Tolerance for Parents of Adolescents" (page 17) and discuss these with the group.

B TEEN PANEL

Before the workshop, assemble a group of three or four teens who are willing to play one of their favorite songs for the workshop participants and to join a panel discussion about the song. Have a tape or CD player ready to play their song. Review the song chosen beforehand to make sure it does not contain crude or vulgar lyrics.

Have the workshop participants ask the teen panel about their choice of this song using the musical chart you've just discussed. Work on getting the teens to respond beyond "I like the music," or "I like the words." Be careful to guide the workshop participants in "positive" questioning.

ASK:

➤ (The workshop participants) **Were any of you attracted to the music? the lyrics? in what way?**

➤ (The teen panel) **What can we do to be more involved in and tolerant of your music?**

CLOSING CONNECTION

SAY:

➤ **Being involved in your teen's musical world can be tough. It's easy to judge and condemn. Taking the time to understand and to listen both to your teen and your teen's music is hard. It takes time and effort to be involved.**

PRAY:

Lord, help us to be a positive and active participant in our teens' growing need for belonging and identity. Help us to gently guide them toward music that will strengthen and encourage them through their teen years. Amen.

LET'S GET ACQUAINTED

1. My parents forbade me to listen to rock and roll. We were only allowed to listen to hymns and choruses.

 ____

2. The first album I bought meant so much to me that I still have it. I can even tell you where I bought it.

 ____

3. I loved listening to my favorite tunes on the radio so much that I often had a small radio under my pillow even after my parents said "lights out."

 ____

4. I can still remember all the details of the first music concert I attended.

 ____

5. I used to dread singing hymns on Sunday morning.

 ____

6. I used to love singing hymns on Sunday morning.

 ____

7. On one or more occasions, my parents made me take back or get rid of an album I bought.

 ____

8. My parents used to yell at me, "Turn it down!"

 ____

9. When my parents weren't home, I'd "crank" up the stereo as loud as I could.

 ____

10. My parents disliked my music.

 ____

11. My parents and I listened to the same music.

 ____

12. When I got angry at someone or something, I turned up my music very loud.

 ____

MUSICAL CHOICES CHART

POPULARITY

This person is compelled ______________________________

____

IDENTITY

Groups or songs ______________________________

____

BELONGING

This person feels ______________________________

____

WORSHIP

Music leads ______________________________

____

REBELLION

A number of causes ______________________________

____

POWER

An actual ______________________________

____

FANTASY

A lack of ______________________________

____

RELAXATION

This person uses ______________________________

____

EXPRESSION

This person ______________________________

____

DISTRACTION

This person uses music ______________________________

____

Musical Choices Worksheet

Match the "motivations" on the left with the definitions on the right.

A. Popularity	1. It's the cool thing to listen to.
B. Identity	2. I've become what I've dreamed of being.
C. Belonging	3. I can play it loud and block everything out.
D. Worship	4. It helps me "chill out."
E. Rebellion	5. I can praise God through songs.
F. Power	6. It allows me to escape the adult world.
G. Fantasy	7. I use music to express myself.
H. Relaxation	8. It fills a void in my life.
I. Expression	9. When I listen, I feel that I can beat the bullies in my life.
J. Distraction	10. I confide in my music and I can relate to it.

THE TWELVE STEPS OF MUSIC TOLERANCE FOR PARENTS OF ADOLESCENTS

1. We admit that we are powerless over our adolescent's musical tastes and choices.
2. We believe that a power greater than ourselves can restore us to sanity.
3. We have made a decision to turn our adolescent's life and musical choices over to the care of God.
4. We have made a searching and fearless inventory of our own musical tastes and choices.
5. We have admitted to God, to ourselves, and to our adolescents all of the musical choices we made in our adolescent years.
6. We are ready to have God remove all of our negative and destructive words and thoughts about our adolescent's musical choices.
7. We have humbly asked our adolescent to allow us into his or her musical world.
8. We have made a list of all the adolescents whom we have prejudged for their musical choices and are willing to make amends with them.
9. We will try to accept such adolescents whenever possible.
10. We continue to take a personal inventory; and when we are prejudiced, judgmental, or condemning, we will promptly admit it.
11. We have sought through prayer to improve our relationship with our adolescent.
12. Having had a musical awakening through the power of God, we have tried to carry this message of acceptance to other parents.

MEDIA: VISIONS, VOICES, AND CHOICES

SESSION 1: MUSIC: REASON BEHIND THE RHYTHM?

SESSION 2: HTTP://WWW.GOD.NET

SESSION 3: THE GOOD, THE BAD, AND THE UGLY—YOU HAVE TO CHOOSE!

Purpose

This unit is designed to help youth explore the content and choices involved in music, television, and the Internet from a Christian perspective.

This Is Not Junk Mail!

IT'S IMPORTANT STUFF FROM YOUR TEENAGER'S SUNDAY MORNING LEADER

CHOICE

The focus of this unit of CONNECT is to help your youth learn to choose wisely. The media competes with you, with the church, and even with God, for your youth's attention. We must help youth get beyond the jingles and the hype to the real message. This unit gives them some skills they can use to distinguish the helpful from the potentially harmful messages. This unit has been written with the belief that music, television, and the Internet are not bad inventions. Rather, they are tools that can be used for entertainment, education, or other positive uses. But they may also be the source of misinformation, violence, and exploitation. The choice is up to the one who holds the remote, buys the CD, or clicks the mouse. The choice is ours.

WARNING: FREEDOM WITHOUT RESPONSIBILITY

Society emphasizes one's right to choose. We argue that people have the right to present their arguments on difficult or controversial topics. We argue for the rights of those who want to live life differently—whatever that may be. It may be a life in seclusion or life of extravagance. We say that the bottom line is "it's their life, their choice."

We have, in fact, so jealously guarded our right to choose that we have failed to consider the consequences of our choices, both for ourselves and for others. What we, as a society, want is complete freedom of choice without any bearing any responsibility for the consequences of our choices. People are free to do whatever they want, without regard to how it may affect themselves or others. To a large extent we have absolved ourselves of the results that our actions may have.

This isn't the Christian way. We have a divinely mandated responsibility to one another—to our neighbors and to our children. Society and the inventions that we have created are not evil in themselves, though they can be put to improper use. As faithful Christians, we exercise our right to choose in a responsible manner both by our use of the media and by the power we allow it to have in our lives. We must ask ourselves, "Does this point me to love and peace? Or does this encourage harm and demean others?" We weigh our choices carefully and prayerfully. Then and only then will freedom be what it was intended to be—a catalyst for experiencing God.

TALK ABOUT IT!

Take time to discuss television (or music, or the Internet) with your youth. Allow this discussion to be a dialogue, not a lecture. You might want to have family members list TV shows that they feel are helpful and shows that they feel are harmful. Discuss the "why" behind each listing. Then create a list of criteria for whether a show should be watched. Decide as a family what is acceptable and what isn't. Everyone will have different interests. Perhaps there is at least one show that the whole family can watch together. Make it a date for the family! Pray for the strength and wisdom to "guard your hearts and minds."

Hallelujah!

IDEAS FOR PEOPLE WHO PLAN WORSHIP

UPBEAT HYMNS

If you know a guitar player in your congregation, work with him or her to "jazz" up some of the older, traditional hymns. Changing the style of music can help the youth more easily identify with the message of the hymn. You might try it with hymns like the following:

"Be Thou My Vision"
"Seek Ye First"
"Amazing Grace"

Other worship songs that are often hits with youth are

"I Will Call Upon the Lord"
"Sanctuary"
"Lord, I Lift Your Name on High"
"Awesome God"

These can be found in many praise compilation books.

COMMITMENT

Invite the youth to write prayers of commitment. Ask them to list the criteria they will use in making wise choices about TV, music, or the Internet. Encourage them to be specific. This may be very personal, especially if they have struggled with this topic before. Give them the opportunity to share their prayer with the group—more importantly, give them time to pray the prayer.

CELEBRATE THE GIFT OF CHOICE!

God has given us the ability to choose. Use the following Scripture passages in worship to emphasize the blessed freedom found in choosing the things of God.

Matthew 5:13
Matthew 6:22-23
Philippians 4:8-9
Joshua 24:14-15

SERMON IDEAS

Matthew 5:13: Jesus says we, as Christians, are like salt for everyone on earth. This may be the time to have some "salty" things in the pulpit like popcorn, chips, or pretzels. The sermon might contrast the appeal of forms of media with the message and life of the church. Why are both inviting? Why do we search for salt in our physical and spiritual lives? Should the church invent new rituals and celebrations that link us with the salty identity Jesus has given us? What might those be? This sermon might get some energetic responses from youth as well as adults.

Joshua 24:14-15: Joshua reminds us that we must make choices about whom we will serve—either the one true God or one of the many false gods and idols. While we may be in little danger of bowing down before golden calves, the temptation to give ultimate power and position to a person (rock star, Hollywood celebrity, or the "coolest" person in school) or thing (money, power, prestige). This sermon might feature a Top Ten List of things, people, and experiences that have become idols for us and explore why they are so attractive to us. Do these idols keep us from a full relationship with Jesus Christ?

Miscellany

IDEAS FOR TEACHERS

YOUTH AND MEDIA: VISIONS, VOICES, AND CHOICES

This unit will discuss three areas of media influence that young people experience: music, television, and the Internet. It looks at the possibilities and limitations of these types of media and will help enable youth to make wise decisions about what they watch, hear, and do.

The main point addressed by this unit is the need for youth to make responsible choices about media. This does not mean they are to deprive themselves of all entertainment. It does, however, mean that whatever we put into our mind deeply affects us. Sometimes that influence is small and sometimes it is large. For example, in the movie "Money Train," a bottle bomb thrown through a booth window kills a subway attendant. Weeks after the release of the movie, the incident was copied in a New York subway. But this time it wasn't acting—it was real life.

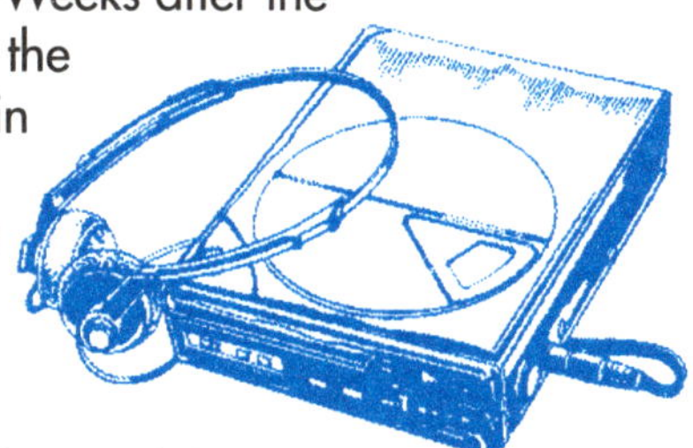

Try to help youth understand that you aren't trying to decide for them what is appropriate and what isn't. Your main role is to help them be wise stewards of the hearts and minds with which God has graced them.

THE COLLECTION

Collect a variety of videos and music for these sessions. Try to find examples of both the best and the worst. Open the sessions with video clips or audio samples. This can help the youth get into the topic a bit easier than starting "cold."

TRUE ALTERNATIVE MUSIC

Some youth, depending on their temperament and age, may be open to listening to and enjoying contemporary Christian music. This genre of music has greatly improved over the past five years. More youth than ever are tuning in. There are many groups that are saying and doing positive things in music and combining it with ministry.

Below are a few examples of contemporary Christian musicians and their work. Keep in mind that popularity is a fleeting thing; some of these artists may be considered "old fashioned" by the time this issue of CONNECT is published. But note especially that not all contemporary Christian music sounds alike; that's why one column lists "Type of Music" and illustrates at least four different styles. If you have some youth who are open to the idea, check out these bands at your local Christian bookstore or discount store.

BAND OR ARTIST	ALBUM	TYPE OF MUSIC
Jars of Clay	*Jars of Clay*	Alternative Acoustic Rock
Steven Curtis Chapman	*Signs of Life*	Rock
The Kry	*What About Now?*	Alternative Rock
Rebecca St. James	*God*	Alternative Rock
Third Day	*Third Day*	Alternative Rock
Susan Ashton	*A Distant Call*	Soft Rock
Carolyn Arends	*I Can Hear You*	Acoustic Rock

SESSION 1:

MUSIC: REASON BEHIND THE RHYTHM?

FOCUS

To examine what values the Christian faith offers in selecting appropriate music to listen to.

SCRIPTURE

Ephesians 4:29

HERE'S THE PLAN DO IT YOUR WAY

OPTIONS	TIME (minutes)	PREPARATION	SUPPLIES
INITIAL CONNECTION			
A All Bands to the Stage!	10	gather supplies	CDs, CD player; OR a copy of Billboard's Top 10 or 20
B It's Not My Kind of Music	10		paper and pencils
CONNECT WITH THE SESSION			
A You Be the Judge!	15	obtain a variety of musical recordings, from your own collection or from a friend (see session plan for more information); preview and select four or five different songs to play for your class	musical recordings on CD or cassette; CD or cassette player
B Motives and Music	10		a large sheet of paper, dry-erase board or chalkboard; markers or chalk
CONNECT WITH THE BIBLE AND THE FAITH COMMUNITY			
A Good Choice?	10		Bibles
B Voices from the Heart	10		Bibles
CONNECT WITH LIFE			
A Hitting the Big Time!	15		paper, pencils or colored markers
B Looking for God Around Us	15		musical recordings (same ones as you used at the beginning of the session); CD or cassette player; a Bible
CLOSING CONNECTION			
A Deserted Island	10		
B Prayer Song: A Song of Prayer	10		hymnals or songbooks; a large sheet of paper and markers; tape
C Praise the Lord!	10		Bibles

INITIAL CONNECTION

A ALL BANDS TO THE STAGE!

> **Desired Result:**
> To start class members thinking about their experience of and preferences for music.

variety of music CDs; at least one CD player; OR a copy of Billboard's Top 10 or 20 in various categories
(Allow 15 minutes.)

Have the youth form teams of no more than four people. Try to mix the group into teams of people who do not usually sit together or spend time together. You might count off by fours or use another way to divide the group members into new teams.

SAY:

➤ **You are a band. It is your job to decide who is the singer, the guitar player, the keyboard player, and drummer. Come up with a name for your "group" and a style of music you would like to play. I have several styles of music here that you can choose from. Pick a song that represents your band.**

Give them time to assign band positions and to choose a name and identity for their bands. As the teams decide who is to be the singer, the drummer, the guitar player, and the keyboard person, ask them to think together as a team why each member is assigned a particular role. Then discuss the following questions as a group:

ASK:

➤ **Who was selected to be the singer and why?**

➤ **How did this selection process take place? Did people volunteer?**

➤ **Did anyone reject the first assignment made by the team?**

➤ **What can the teams learn from this simple exercise?**

DISCUSS:

➤ **Why did you choose that particular type of music for your band?**

➤ **How did you choose your name?**

➤ **To what extent can you identify with the music or the words?**

Listen to their reasons!

B IT'S NOT MY KIND OF MUSIC

paper and pencils
(Allow 10 minutes.)

Set up a mock debate by dividing your group into four teams. Assign one team "rock music," a second team "classical music," a third team "country music," and the fourth team "rap music." Give each team two minutes to present an argument proving that its musical style is the very best type of music.

After the four teams have made their initial presentations each team will have one minute to respond to any of the other three statements or to continue to argue for its own kind of music. Allow the teams time to meet to determine who their spokespersons will be and what arguments those spokespersons will use.

Conduct the mock debate and anticipate some laughter! Do not let this become a shouting match, however.

DISCUSS:

➤ **Who determines what is good music, and how?**

➤ **What makes music good or bad?**

➤ **How can persons be helped to respect one another's taste in music?**

➤ **How can persons learn to appreciate—or at least tolerate—another's taste in music?**

CONNECT WITH THE SESSION

Desired Result: To help youth begin thinking about music in relation to values. **(Choose Option A or B.)**

A YOU BE THE JUDGE!

musical recordings on CD or cassette; CD player or cassette player ***(Allow 15 minutes.)***

Obtain a variety of recordings from your own collection or from a friend. You don't have to particularly like the music! Be sure to incorporate music that is currently popular. It may be worthwhile to look at the Billboard Top 10 and purchase a few cassette singles for this purpose. Pick four or five very different songs and play them for the youth.

SAY:

➤ **Rate each of these songs, based on the following ratings scale:**

A=excellent; B=good; C=average; D=no good; E=eject it now!

ASK:

➤ **What did you base your ratings on** (musical style, lyrics, beat, etc.)**?**

B MOTIVES AND MUSIC

a large sheet of paper, dry-erase board or chalkboard; markers or chalk ***(Allow 10 minutes.)***

People write music for a variety of reasons. Often composers want to express creatively what they have felt or experienced. Since nearly everyone has been in love at one time or another, love songs are almost always popular. The following exercises are designed to help the youth look beneath the surface of the music itself to the motives of the composer of the lyrics and music.

Have the youth to discuss one or more of the following questions:

ASK:

➤ **What are your favorite bands or artists? Why?**

➤ **What would be the perfect band? Who would be in it? Why?**

➤ **Why do you think people write music?**

➤ **Why do some play heavy metal, some rap, some blues, some instrumental?**

➤ **To what extent, and in what ways, are lyrics important? Why or why not?**

Record the group's responses on the board or on a large sheet of paper.

CONNECT WITH THE BIBLE AND THE FAITH COMMUNITY

A GOOD CHOICE?

Desired Result:
To examine the relation of the values offered by the Bible and the Christian faith to the musical preferences of youth.
(Choose Option A or B.)

Bibles
(Allow 10 minutes.)

Invite volunteers to read aloud the following Scripture passages:

- **First Chronicles 15:16** (It's in the middle of the Old Testament between 2 Kings and Ezra.)
- **Ephesians 4:29**
- **Matthew 6:22-23** (You may ask them to substitute "ears" for "eyes.")

ASK:

➤ **Why did David command the people to play music?** (1 Chronicles 15:16)

SAY:

➤ **Did you ever think of cooking as a metaphor for checking what goes into our heads? They both depend on careful choices about what is included. In order for either to have any benefit they have to have good ingredients.**

ASK:

➤ **If we were going to make a hamburger what would we want to use? What types of ingredients or seasonings?** (See if they can name some seasonings. Then offer ridiculous ideas such as marshmallows, licorice, turnip greens, liver.)

DISCUSS:

➤ **Just as it is important to pick good ingredients to make a good hamburger, it is important to put good ingredients in our minds.** (Read Ephesians 4:29.) **We have a lot of music to choose from. How can we use Ephesians 4:29 to help us make wise choices?**

➤ According to what Jesus said in the Matthew passage we looked at, why is it important to make choices carefully about what we see or hear?

➤ Name some songs or bands that you think are a good choice to listen to. Why did you choose them?

Bibles
(Allow 10 minutes.)

B VOICES FROM THE HEART

SAY:

➤ **David is a very popular musician in the Bible. He played the harp, sang, and composed music. He used music to talk about his feelings of God. People, years later, still use his words, the Psalms, to talk about their faith.**

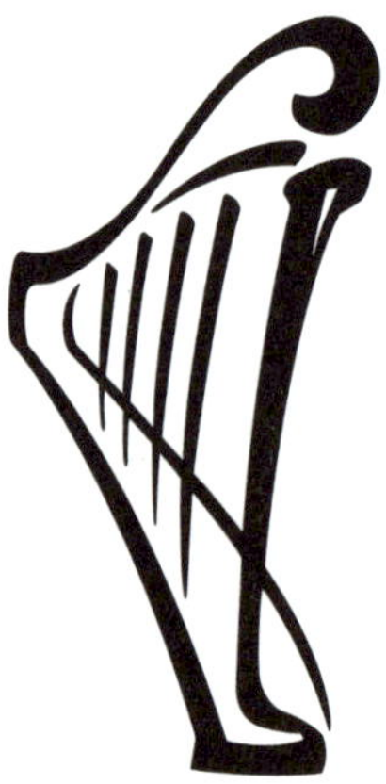

Ask several youth to read aloud the following passages:

- **Psalm 4:8**
- **Psalm22:1-2**
- **Psalm 105:1-2**

DISCUSS:

➤ **How are these psalms different? Compare what they are saying.**

➤ **What do you think David was feeling as he wrote each of the three passages?**

➤ **Why do you think people might read these three passages today?**

➤ **When you feel down, what kind of music do you choose to listen to? Why?**

➤ **When you are in a good mood, what kind of music do you choose to listen to? Why?**

Desired Result:
To help youth begin to connect Christian values with real-life choices like what music they will listen to.
(Choose Option A or B.)

paper, pencils or colored markers
(Allow 15 minutes.)

CONNECT WITH LIFE

A HITTING THE BIG TIME!

SAY:

➤ **Please return to the same teams that were formed at the beginning of this session. Each team is a band consisting of a singer, guitarist, keyboard player, and drummer. You even picked out a name for your group and a style of music for your group! Your task now is to discuss and describe the kinds of messages your music will convey. What do you want your music to do for others? What effect do you want your music to have on its hearers? How can you be sure that the music has the effect you intended?**

Give the teams several minutes to discuss these issues, then have each team report to the group. Help the group come to realize the potential for good—or harm—that music can have.

B LOOKING FOR GOD AROUND US

musical recordings (same ones as you used at the beginning of the session); CD or cassette player; a Bible
(Allow 15 minutes.)

Spirituality doesn't need to be stuffy! Ask each youth to go through the musical recordings you brought and find his or her favorite. Some will obviously have to live with the leftovers!

Ask someone to read aloud Ephesians 4:29.

SAY:

➤ **With the music you have, grade the lyrics and music based on Ephesians 4:29. If the lyrics fail the test, rewrite the section that failed. Make sure the song does not "tear down" anyone.**

Allow time for class members to complete this task. Ask several volunteers to describe the music they chose and to indicate if the lyrics passed the Ephesians 4:29 test. If the lyrics failed the test, how did the volunteers rewrite them to make them more acceptable?

ASK:

➤ **What difference does the music we listen to make to us or to anyone else?**

➤ **How does what music you hear in the privacy of your own room or car affect other people?**

➤ **Isn't listening to music a private, personal thing? Why should anyone care what music you choose?**

Help the members of your group begin to understand the subtle power and influence of music and the ways it can indirectly affect other people through the values and belief systems that are shaped and influenced by the music the youth listen to.

SAY:

➤ **Based on what we have read and discussed, in what ways will you think twice about your choices in music? Why or why not?**

Desired Result: To offer class members an opportunity to choose.

(Allow 10 minutes.)

CLOSING CONNECTION

A DESERTED ISLAND

Ask group members to think about the values discussed in this session.

ASK:

➤ **If you were stranded on a deserted island with nothing but a CD player and one CD, what CD would you want to have with you? Why?**

Stand as a group in a large circle. Ask each person what CD they chose. Now ask the group members to divide quickly into teams of four.

SAY:

➤ **Suppose your team of four were stranded on a deserted island with nothing but a CD player and one CD. You four know that you will have to start civilization all over again. What CD will you choose, and why? What CD would assist the four of you in remembering and rebuilding the values of civilization?**

This is a tough question, but it goes to the heart of the importance of music and the emotions, attitudes, and values it can foster in persons. Don't expect immediate responses; give the teams time to think and to discuss the issue.

Ask teams to make a brief report. Close with this prayer or one of your own:

> **Great and gracious God: Thank you for the possibility of making choices and for your guidance in making those choices. Help us to make the right choices at home, at school, and in all of our living. In Jesus' name, we pray. Amen.**

hymnals or songbooks; a large sheet of paper and markers; tape ***(Allow 10 minutes.)***

B A PRAYER SONG: A SONG OF PRAYER

Distribute copies of your church's hymnal or copies of contemporary Christian songbooks. Ask group members, working in pairs, to look for examples of "prayer songs," hymns or songs whose words are actually prayers. Ask the pairs to write a brief prayer, using lines from at least three different hymns or songs. Invite the pairs to write their prayers on large sheets of paper and to fasten these to the walls of your room so that all can see them.

Have the group stand in a circle, join hands, and ask several of the pairs to offer their prayers aloud.

PRAISE THE LORD!

Tell the group members that you are going to read a psalm aloud, one line at a time, and you want them to repeat the line back to you in unison. But here's the trick. They must repeat the line just as you said it. The psalm is a wonderful song of joy, Psalm 150. Here is this Psalm from *The New Revised Standard Version of the Bible*; feel free to use the translation or version you usually use in your group. Throw caution to the wind as you read this psalm aloud and encourage your class members to repeat the lines after you. Read each line with as much expression—even exaggerated expression—as you can. Try to make your words sound like the instruments described in the psalm. Along with the words of this Psalm, here are some suggestions for how to say each line. You may want to practice a few times before the session.

Praise the Lord! *(Say this loudly!)*
Praise God in his sanctuary, *(Emphasize the words "praise" and "his.")*
Praise God in his mighty firmament! *(The firmament is all that God has created; stretch out the words "his," "mighty," and "firmament." Emphasize "mighty.")*
Praise him for his mighty deeds; *(Come down hard on the word "mighty," say it as two equal syllables: "MY-TEA")*
Praise him according to his surpassing greatness! *(Emphasize "him" here, and stretch out "surpassing.")*
Praise him with trumpet sound; *(Say "trumpet sound" like the words were coming out of a trumpet: "TRUM-PET SOUND".)*
Praise him with lute and harp! *(Make your voice lilt and dance and sing here.)*
Praise him with strings and pipe! *(Stretch out the words "strings" and "pipe.")*
Praise him with clanging cymbals! *(Make your voice "clang" with those cymbals!)*
Praise him with loud clashing cymbals! *(Go ahead and shout! Make every one in the whole building hear those "loud clashing cymbals" that are praising God!)*
Let everything that breathes praise the Lord! *(Emphasize "praise the Lord.")*
Praise the Lord! *(Vibrate the walls on this one; shout, "Praise the Lord!" like you really mean it!)*

Help your group members understand that God deserves all our praise, that all that we have and all that we are is a gift of God's love. Invite the group members to stand in a circle, join hands, and to silently thank God for the persons standing on their right and on their left. Close with a prayer thanking God for each of the members of your class. Praise God aloud for the particular gift each teen brings to the group.

Read Me

THIS IS WHAT YOU NEED TO KNOW ABOUT THE TOPIC.

KEY VERSE

Do not let any unwholesome talk come out of your mouths, but only what is helpful for building others up according to their needs, that it may benefit those who listen.
Ephesians 4:29 (NIV)

Music is a strong influence in the lives of youth today. The popularity of MTV and VH1 and the enormous amount of money youth spend on music demonstrate this fact. Music can greatly influence on our moods. People often use music to pick them up emotionally or to console them when they are "down." Because youth so often feel alone and misunderstood, they may be prone to choose music that is viewed as non-conformist precisely because it is strange, bewildering, and somewhat frightening to adults. Rock music, in particular, has a history of this.

Whatever your opinion of rock and roll, a new type of violent music is now popular among some youth: "shock rock." Its popularity is bewildering to many. It apparently is part of the increasing trend of popularity toward "shock." Think of the many ways within popular culture that "shock sells." At its core, this type of music is offensive. This offensiveness can be found in the lyrics, but can also be witnessed in the behavior of bands at some concerts. Some bands even express great disdain and hatred for God and all that the church stands for. Other bands are known for vulgarity and obscenity of the grossest kinds. But not all bands are this way. Some perform music that is genuinely entertaining and fun.

For many teens, this difference can be difficult to discern. Things that are different or odd are often strangely appealing, especially for youth This session attempts to help give youth faithful decision-making skills and tools so that they will learn to choose music that doesn't glamorize things that are harmful and sinful.

Realize that your youth will ultimately have to make their own choices. We cannot make it for them. But we can influence the choices that youth make by setting good examples. More importantly, we can talk with youth about our Christian values and how to make choices based on these values. Above all, we must love our youth and encourage them to be good stewards of the heart and mind that God has given them.

FOOD *for* THOUGHT

As adults, we must avoid expecting or demanding immediate change in a teen's (or anyone else's) Christian life. We must trust that God will be present to help a person understand what is hurtful and to help him or her grow and mature in faith.

Too often, we focus on the outward characteristics of our youth and judge a teen's spirituality or Christian maturity based on these characteristics. For example, the fine, upstanding young man who wears his hair neatly and always dresses appropriately, who drives slowly and carefully and has the sign of the fish on his car bumper, and who sits quietly in church every Sunday morning may look like a model Christian. But inwardly, his spiritual life may be in turmoil and his faith shaky and uncertain. On the other hand, the "rebel" or the non-conformist about whom everyone is concerned because of the casual way she dresses and sometimes acts may be a person who is firmly rooted in a strong personal faith in Christ.

Our job is simply to love our teens. Love them now, just as they are. Take the risk of sincerely telling them, in words and actions, that you love them. And when you do, God will be present and will become increasingly real to that teen because you showed her or him unconditional love: that kind of love can come only from God.

JESUS AND THE PARTY

Did you know that Jesus was not boring? Really! Many people think he was solemn-faced and told people what they could not and should not do. Nothing could be farther from the truth!

Would you invite Jesus to a party? If you wanted to have fun, would you invite someone who hated to have fun? No way! But people did invite him and the disciples to parties.

If you want to read about a party that Jesus and the disciples attended, just look at John's account of Jesus and the disciples at the wedding at Cana (John 2:1-12). In Jesus' time weddings were huge parties, just like they are today! If he had been a drag, no one would have wanted him around. Jesus wasn't any less God when he was at the party. He just had to show us that spirituality doesn't have to be stuffy!

Not only did Jesus like to go to parties, he liked to throw parties for his friends and to talk about parties and celebrations. Take a look at the fifteenth chapter of the Gospel of Luke and notice that it is full of images of things that were at one time lost, but were later found: lost sheep, a lost coin, and two lost sons. What happens when these are found? Jesus says that the people who found them threw parties for all their friends! The shepherd called his friends to a party because he had found the sheep. The woman found her coin, called in her neighbors, and had a party! And the father held a big celebration when one of his sons came home and the other one came to his senses. Notice how Jesus ends these stories: he talks of the joy in heaven when even "one sinner repents!"

Every time you and I make a decision for Jesus Christ, every time you and I decide to follow Christ rather than the crowd, every time you and I make a new commitment to live as disciples of Jesus Christ, heaven is filled with joy and the party preparations increase!

Would you want Jesus at one of your parties? (Hint: That's an unfair question. He's already there!)

Hey! Copy this page for your youth—really, we want you to!

YOUTHPAGE

HEAVEN IN THE REAL WORLD

BY STEPHEN CURTIS CHAPMAN

These lyrics were written to encourage and uplift. Think about the words. Do they remind you that God is here with you—in the real world?

I saw it again today in the face of a little child
Looking through eyes of fear and uncertainty
It echoed in a cry for freedom across the street and across the miles
Cries from the heart, to find the missing part.

Chorus

Where is the hope? Where is the peace?
That will make this life complete
For every man, woman, boy and girl
Looking for Heaven in the real world
To stand in the pouring rain and believe the sun will shine again
To know that the grave is not the end
To feel the embrace of grace and cross the line where real life begins
And know in your heart you've found the missing part.

Chorus

There is a hope. There is a peace.
That will make this life complete
For every man, woman, boy and girl
Looking for Heaven in the real world
Heaven in the real world.

Bridge

It happened one night with a tiny baby's birth
God heard creation crying and He sent Heaven to Earth.

Chorus

He is the hope. He is the peace.
That will make this life complete
For every man, woman, boy and girl
Looking for Heaven in the real world
Heaven in the real world.

SESSION 2:
HTTP://WWW.GOD.NET

FOCUS

To examine what values the Christian faith offers for making responsible choices while surfing the World Wide Web.

SCRIPTURE

Galatians 5:22-23

HERE'S THE PLAN **DO IT YOUR WAY**

OPTIONS	TIME (minutes)	PREPARATION	SUPPLIES
INITIAL CONNECTION			
A Web Mania	10	obtain a large map of the world or make a rough sketch on a large sheet of paper or a board; read some basic information about the World Wide Web in a book or magazine	large map of the world; or butcher paper and markers or dry erase board and markers; sticky notes
CONNECT WITH THE SESSION			
A Caution! It Can Be a Maze Out There!	10	make copies of YouthPage	YouthPage, pencils, newsprint, markers
B It's a Matter of Focus	15	purchase several bags of multicolored candies; obtain bowls, ladles, and spoons	bags of multicolored candies (M&M®, Skittles®, or jelly beans); 2 large bowls; 2 identical ladles or scoops; 2 small spoons
CONNECT WITH THE BIBLE AND FAITH COMMUNITY			
A Freedom to Choose	15		Bibles
B Fruity Charades	15	read Galatians 5:16-18, 22-26; write down a different "fruit" of the spirit on enough slips of paper for each student you anticipate might be in class	Bibles, slips of paper listing fruits of the spirit
CONNECT WITH LIFE			
A To Click or Not to Click	15	read the NOTE TO THE TEACHER that appears in the session plan	paper, colored pencils or markers
B Design Your Own Web Site!	15		paper, colored pencils or markers
C Surf Some "Good Fruit" Sites	20	arrange for a computer with Internet access to be available; get someone to help you set up and "surf" if you are not familiar with the Internet	a desktop or laptop computer with modem and Internet access
CLOSING CONNECTION			
A Choosing "Good Fruit"	10	prepare several bowls of fruit to place on tables in the classroom	either the "homepages" drawn by the youth earlier in this session or printouts of websites that you have visited; bowls of fruit

Desired Result:
To answer initial questions about the Internet, and to start class members thinking about their experiences with the World Wide Web.

large map of the world or either butcher paper and markers or dry erase board and markers; sticky notes
(Allow 10 minutes.)

INITIAL CONNECTION

WEB MANIA

Obtain a large map of the world. If you cannot find one, do your best artistic impression on large butcher paper, chalkboard, or dry-erase board. Place the map where all of the youth can see it, and give each person a small sticky note.

SAY:

➤ **If you could go any place in the world, where would you go?**

Invite each youth to write his or her name on a sticky note and post it on the area of the world he or she would like to visit.

SAY:

➤ **What is the Internet? Could it allow you to visit these places? How?**

Desired Result:
To help youth begin thinking about choices that may be involved with using the Internet.
(Choose Option A or B.)

YouthPage, pencils; a large sheet of paper and markers
(Allow 10 minutes.)

CONNECT WITH THE SESSION

CAUTION! IT CAN BE A MAZE OUT THERE!

A

SAY:

➤ **The Internet can be a lot like a maze—just like the one on the YouthPage. Many people sign on and wander through until they find something of interest. Sometimes they make wise choices that help them learn, grow, or entertain themselves. But people also make poor choices that lead to dead ends, confusion, or worse.**

Have the youth complete the maze on the YouthPage.

ASK:

➤ **What are some possible poor choices you might make when you are using the Internet?**

➤ **What makes these poor choices?**

➤ **How can you make better choices?**

Record the group's answers on the board or on a large sheet of papers.

IT'S A MATTER OF FOCUS

Put several bags of multicolored candies (such as M&M's®, Skittles®, or jelly beans) into 2 large bowls. Have the youth form two teams, one red and one green. Give each team a ladle or scoop.

several bags of multicolored candies (such as M&M's®, Skittles®, or jelly beans; 2 large bowls; 2 identical ladles or scoops; 2 small spoons ***(Allow 15 minutes.)***

SAY:

➤ **Try to scoop as many candies as you can from the bowl that match your team's color as possible. You may make as many scoops as you want, but once you pull the ladle from the bowl, all the candies on the ladle must be removed. At the end of one minute we will tally up the number of green candies the green team collected and the number of red candies the red team collected. BUT: We will subtract the number of other colored candies from each team's total. For example, if the red team has twenty red candies in its pile, but also has six green, three brown (or purple), five yellow, and two blue, its score is 4.**

Have them complete the contest.

ASK:

➤ **You were as careful as you could be. Why did you still end up with other colors of candies?**

➤ **How could you have avoided this? Explain.**

Now give each team a small spoon.

SAY:

➤ **We will now change the game. Use the spoon to do the same task.**

After the teams have completed this second challenge,

DISCUSS:

➤ **Did using the spoon make a difference? Why? What could you do with the small spoon that you could not do with the scoop?**

➤ **If the candies represent the choices we make, what does this tell us about how we should approach each choice?**

Desired Result:
To examine values offered by the Bible and the Christian faith that may be relevant to using the World Wide Web.
(Choose Option A or B.)

Bibles
(Allow 15 minutes.)

CONNECT WITH THE BIBLE AND FAITH COMMUNITY

A FREEDOM TO CHOOSE

SAY:

➤ **So much of who and what we are is a result of our choices. Our choices are often determined by those things that we consider most important and are most focused on. To what extent are we focused on God and what God loves? And to what extent are we caught up in what is simply popular or "in?" These passages encourage us to keep our focus and attention on God.**

Invite the youth to look up and read the following:

- **Romans 12:2**
- **Luke 6:43**
- **Galatians 5:16-18, 22-26.**

DISCUSS:

➤ **These passages talk a lot about fruit. What does the image of fruit represent? If you were rewriting these passages, what image might you choose instead of fruit?**

➤ **The writer of Galatians lists nine "fruits of the spirit." What additional "fruits of the spirit" might the writer have used? Can you think of at least three more positive "fruits of the spirit"?**

SAY:

➤ **Bad fruit affects not only the owner of the tree, but everyone who eats that fruit. This image suggests that if we make bad choices, other people are affected by those choices. Give some examples of times when your bad choices have affected others or times when you have been affected by the bad choices of another person.**

B FRUITY CHARADES

Bibles; prepared slips of paper with "fruits" of the spirit ***(Allow 15 minutes.)***

Ask one or two volunteers to read aloud Luke 6:43-45 and Galatians 5:16-18, 22-26 while the rest of the group members follow along in their Bibles. List on the chalkboard or a large sheet of paper the nine fruits of the spirit described in the passage from Galatians. Assign a fruit of the spirit to each person by handing out the slips of paper you had prepared in advance. Tell the class not to share what is printed on their slips.

SAY:

➤ **The Galatians passage talks about fruits of the spirit. These are ways of acting that show our love and devotion to God. You each are to act out the fruit of the spirit listed on the slip of paper I have given you without using any words. Everyone else will try to guess what fruit you are!**

Let each person take a turn acting out his or her "fruit."

SAY:

➤ **Now, pick a "bad fruit" or way of acting that is contrary to one of the fruits of the Spirit. Act it out and we will try to guess what it is.**

Let each person take a turn acting out a "bad fruit."

SAY:

➤ **We all know "good" fruit when we see it. We all know "bad" fruit when we see it.**

ASK:

➤ **Why is choosing good fruit instead of bad fruit sometimes difficult?**

➤ **What are some of the prices we may have to pay in order to choose good fruit?** (If group members have trouble at this point, remind them of costs such as losing popularity with some other youth, being viewed as different, or being ridiculed by other teens.)

➤ **Can we always tell in advance which is the good fruit and which is the bad fruit? Give some examples to illustrate your answer.**

➤ **What can we do to help us choose good fruit?**

➤ **In what ways do our choices affect others around us? Give some examples.**

Desired Result:
To help youth begin to connect Christian values with real-life choices in the Internet websites they choose to view.
(Choose Option A, B, or C)

paper and colored pencils or markers
(Allow 15 minutes.)

CONNECT WITH LIFE

A

TO CLICK OR NOT TO CLICK

NOTE TO THE TEACHER:
This option includes several Internet website URLs (URL = Uniform Resource Locator: this is the address you type into your web browser to call up a particular website). At the time this publication was written and edited, some of the websites were real and some were fictitious. However, the content of the World Wide Web and the Internet changes greatly on a daily basis. Approach any website with caution. Before class, you might want to test where any URLs really do take you and decide whether they are appropriate to share with your class members.

Also note that some of the website URLs listed below may obviously appear to be inappropriate sites for Christian youth to visit. Use your best judgment whether you wish to use this option with your particular group of youth. However, we believe that the only way youth will learn to apply Christian values to real-life choices is by discussing what criteria they will use to judge whether a particular website is appropriate for them to view.

SAY:
➤ **When we use the Internet, some sites will get our attention. Some of the sites we can access are not going to be "good fruit." If you had the following websites on a menu on your computer, would you click your way into the site, or click your way out? Why? What do you think you would find that would make you want to stay or leave?**

- **www.mtv.com**
- **www.sports.com**
- **www.flirts.com**
- **www.poetscorner.com**
- **www.dogsandcats.com**
- **www.algebra.com**
- **www.playboy.com**
- **www.worldtravel.com**
- **www.dealingwithparents.com**
- **www.cults.com**

SAY:

➤ **Name some "good fruit" sites that you have seen on the Internet. Use a sheet of paper to draw the homepage of some good fruit sites. If you can't remember what the homepage looks like, design it for them!!**

Post the drawings of homepages around the room.

B DESIGN YOUR OWN WEBSITE!

paper, colored pencils or markers
(Allow 15 minutes.)

On a sheet of paper (regular 8½ x 11 will do) have the youth design their own web page. The only criteria is that it must in some way be a "good fruit" site. Otherwise, it can be anything they desire. Ask them to come up with a theme, a site address, and why they think that it would be a good site to have on the Internet. Ask youth to post the websites around the room and to explain their site to the group.

For follow-up: If you have access to the Internet, see if there are any sites similar to the ones the youth designed. If so, give the youth the net address and encourage them to visit the site.

C SURF SOME "GOOD FRUIT" SITES

a desktop or laptop computer with modem; access to an Internet service provider
(Allow at least 20 minutes.)

With supervision from yourself or another adult, surf some safe, "good fruit" sites on the Internet. Discuss what makes them appropriate sites. Among the sites (in operation at the time of the editing and publication of this resource) you might explore are:

- **www.umc.org** (United Methodist information)
- **www.upperroom.org/devozine/default.html** (*Devo'zine* is a devotional magazine designed by and for youth.)
- **www.upperroom.org/emmaus/chrysalis.html** (Chrysalis is a spiritual experience for youth sponsored by The Upper Room.)
- **www.umc.org/action.html** (Click on "Youth" for websites maintained by a number of church youth groups. These sites might give your youth an idea for creating and maintaining their own Internet website.)

Either the homepages drawn by the youth earlier in this session, or printouts of websites that you have visited (good websites to print out and use are those listed in "Surf Some 'Good Fruit' Sites."); several bowls of fruit ***(Allow 10 minutes.)***

> ***Teacher Note:***
>
> One of these activities called for the members of your group to design their own websites or homepages. One or more of these websites may not represent "good fruit" in every case. Encourage your youth to be creative, but describe and discuss how websites designed to shock, to stimulate, or to raise doubts and questions about values may not be sites that bear "good fruit." If you find some of the student-created websites to be questionable (or even objectionable!), engage the whole group in coming up with a list of criteria for evaluating a website (or a magazine or novel or a television program). Keep in mind the Scripture passages considered in this session.

CLOSING CONNECTION

CHOOSING "GOOD FRUIT"

SAY:

- **You are faced with many different choices. Your use of the Internet is just one of these choices. But we all need to be careful that what we put into our minds and hearts is only "good fruit."**

ASK:

- **How would you answer those who say that viewing some "bad fruit" Internet sites does not really affect them at all?**
- **What short-term and long-term effects might visiting "bad fruit" sites on the Internet have—both for the person doing the visiting and for others around that person?**
- **How does what we read, see, and hear influence what we believe, value, and trust?**

Collect the websites or homepages that were created by the members of the group in the previous activity. Place them on tables around the room, with a small bowl of fruit at each "website." Invite the group members to walk around to visit the websites and to enjoy some of the good fruit at each site.

Close this session with a time of prayer. You might offer a prayer, or ask a group member to do so. Include in the prayer the recognition that identifying potentially good and bad fruit is not always easy at first glance, that each of us needs God's help in making choices, and that each of us needs to be committed to choosing the good and rejecting the bad.

Close the prayer time by asking the youth to stand in a circle and join hands while you pray for each youth by name.

Read Me

THIS IS WHAT YOU NEED TO KNOW ABOUT THE TOPIC.

SURF'S UP!! INTERNET 101

The Internet has gained a lot of momentum in the last few years. Online services such as America Online, CompuServe, MSN, Mindspring, Earthlink, and others have had huge increases in users. Computers are becoming common household items, and youth are spending more and more time using them.

America Online (AOL) and CompuServe are the two most common Internet service providers at the writing of this resource. They provide software (computer programs) that enable the user to access the Internet. Usually the software is free; however, there is a usage fee once you sign on. (AOL costs approximately $20 a month for unlimited usage at the time of the writing of this resource.) Once you sign on, the software will guide you to the places you wish to go on the Internet. These services often allow you to place blocks on questionable material, causing certain places to be inaccessible. However, the average computer user can find a way around the blocks.

You may find it beneficial to discuss with your youth ways of limiting time spent surfing the net and the types of sites they will access. Take time to discuss openly the pros and cons of the web.If you are interested in learning more about the Internet, check out any of the myriad Internet books and magazines available in your local bookstore.

BIBLE.COM

Listed below are some biblical passages that warn us to be careful about what we expose ourselves to. Note that each of these references is found in the context of a larger story or narrative. Pulling a verse or two out of context can be dangerous and can lead to misinterpretation.

Matthew 6:22-23: This passage is in the middle of Jesus' Sermon on the Mount. He places these words in the midst of general instructions for living in harmony with God, with the world, and with others.

Some authorities suggest that Jesus uses "eye" in this passage as a metaphor for what we see or give our attention to. If we give our attention to the things of God, our whole body (our life!) will be filled with the light of God's presence.

Mark 14:38: These words, spoken when Jesus was about to be arrested in the Garden of Gethsemane, refer directly to the disciples' temptation to ignore the plight of Jesus and failure to catch the significance of this night in the Garden. But these words can also serve to remind us of how easily we are tempted.

Luke 6:45: The Sermon on the Mount (found in Matthew) is partially repeated in Luke's Gospel, known here as the Sermon on the Plain. Jesus emphasizes that our lives and actions reflect what is within us. We may try to do otherwise, but inevitably our inner selves will dictate our external actions. If we strive to follow God within, our lives will show it. If we only pretend to follow God outwardly, eventually our actions will betray us.

Romans 12:2: Paul is never one to "beat around the bush." In his great letter to Rome, he flatly declares that each of us has the choice to conform to the world or to conform to the things of God. When he talks of the "renewal of the mind," Paul refers to the centering of our heart and soul on the things of God. Paul's summons echoes the Old Testament's call to love God with all our heart, soul, and might (Deuteronomy 6:4), a call to which Christ added loving God with all our "mind" (Matthew 22:37 and parallels).

Ephesians 5:1-20: In this passage, Paul explains in detail the dangers and pitfalls of conformity to the world. How does he suggest we overcome those temptations? His answer is in the first verses: be imitators of God and walk in love.

THE INTERNET MAZE

Hey! Copy this page for your youth—really, we want you to!

> ***The fruit of the Spirit is love, joy, peace, patience, kindness, generosity, faithfulness, gentleness, and self-control. There is no law against these things.***
> ***Galatians 5:22-23***

Like this maze, the Internet can be fun. But there are times when we can lose our focus and take a turn that we'll later regret.

In the space below, list some places that you try to steer clear from on the Internet.

SESSION 3:

THE GOOD, THE BAD, AND THE UGLY: YOU HAVE TO CHOOSE!

FOCUS

To explore what values the Christian faith offers us for making appropriate choices about the television shows we watch.

SCRIPTURE

Philippians 4:8

HERE'S THE PLAN | DO IT YOUR WAY

OPTIONS	TIME (minutes)	PREPARATION	SUPPLIES
INITIAL CONNECTION			
A You Make the Call!	10	prepare index cards with the names of cable television networks	index cards
B The Best and the Worst	15	write numbers from 1 to 50 on a large sheet of paper	large sheet of paper; several markers; masking tape
CONNECT WITH THE SESSION			
A Network Execs	15	Arrange chairs in a circle or use a large table and chairs to create a conference room	
B Under the Influence?	10		
CONNECT WITH THE BIBLE AND FAITH COMMUNITY			
A Are You Watching Where You Are Going?	15		Bibles
CONNECT WITH LIFE			
A Sensitivity Check	10		
B Switch or Stay?	10	using two cards, print the word "switch" on one side of each card and the word "stay" on the other	Two cardboard cards or index cards
CLOSING CONNECTION			
Prayers	10		paper and pencils

INITIAL CONNECTION

A YOU MAKE THE CALL!

Desired Result:
To start class members thinking about the variety of programs available to watch on television.

index cards
(Allow 10 minutes.)

Before the session, print the names of various cable television networks on index cards. Some that you might include are:

- TNT
- ESPN
- HBO
- Cinemax
- Public Television
- Discovery Channel
- Lifetime
- Odyssey
- History Channel
- Playboy Channel
- American Movie Classics

Tell the youth to put the cards in order from healthy to harmful. Group members may ask what you mean by "healthy" and "harmful." Reply that you want them to struggle with that definition and set of criteria. What do the group members think is healthy and harmful, and why?

They must work together on this. When they are finished, ask them to discuss why they made the choices they did.

B THE BEST AND WORST

large sheet of paper; several markers; masking tape
(Allow 15 minutes.)

On a large sheet of paper, list the numbers from 1 to 50, leaving space beside the numbers to fill in the name of the cable network found on that channel.

SAY:

➤ **Pretend this is a list of channel numbers on your television set. How many of these numbers can you identify? For example, which channel is NBC, which is ESPN, which is the Disney Channel, and so on? If you can't identify all the channels by name, can you list some programs you like to watch on several different channels?**

Allow time for the class to work together to fill in the television channel names.

SAY:

➤ **Which of these channels do you think are the best five? Which ones are the worst five?**

Allow everyone to have a say. Make sure to let the youth define what they mean by "best" and "worst" for themselves. Discuss what criteria each person used to determine which channels were among the best and which among the worst.

CONNECT WITH THE SESSION

Desired Result: To help youth begin thinking about choices involved in watching television. **(Choose Option A or B.)**

(Allow 15 minutes.)

A NETWORK EXECS

Arrange the chairs in the room to look like a meeting room. If you have a table, put the chairs around the table to resemble an executive conference room.

SAY:

➤ **You are all members of the board of directors for a network. You are charged with determining the programming for a season. You can choose any programming, but you must fill each category with at least three shows per week. For example, what are the three best shows for the family? for seniors? for young adults? You can use existing shows or make up shows that you wish were on TV. The categories are:**

- **Family**
- **Children** (6-10 years old)
- **Youth** (10-18 years old)
- **Young Adult** (18-25 years old)
- **Adult**
- **Seniors**

Group members may need to be prompted on some of the categories.

ASK:

➤ **Why did you choose each of these shows for each particular audience?**

➤ **Did you have trouble choosing shows for any of the categories? If so, why?**

(Allow 10 minutes.)

B UNDER THE INFLUENCE?

SAY:

➤ **Some people feel that television can have a harmful effect on people. Others say that television can be a positive influence. There is evidence for both of these opinions. What programs do you think may have a** good influence on you? What programs do you think might not be such a great idea to watch? Why?

➤ To what extent does your faith and your understanding of God's will help determine which programs have a positive influence and which have a negative influence? Or is this just a matter of personal taste?

CONNECT WITH THE BIBLE AND THE FAITH COMMUNITY

Desired Result: To help youth begin thinking about the criteria they should use to make wise choices.

ARE YOU WATCHING WHERE YOU ARE GOING?

Bibles
(Allow 15 minutes.)

Have the youth read Colossians 2:8, Genesis 1:31, and Matthew 5:13.

SAY:

➤ **There are several different, yet connected ideas in these passages. In Colossians, we are cautioned not to let ourselves be led astray by ideas that "sound good" and "seem to make sense." In Genesis we are told that after God finished creating the world, God saw "that it was good."**

ASK:

➤ **If all that God created is good, then why are we concerned about TV? If we are good creations of God, how can TV be bad?**

➤ **Can TV (or anything else for that matter) lead us astray? How about friends?**

NOTE TO THE TEACHER! Help the group members struggle with the concept of free will here. While all that God created is good, we have the power (given to us by God!) to refuse to honor and respect all that God has made and to use it for our own selfish ends. God has made everything good, but we can and do corrupt God's creation—including ourselves!

SAY:

➤ **One of the many uses of salt is as a preservative. Salt can be used to keep things from going bad, from spoiling, or from becoming contaminated. Jesus declares that we are the salt of the earth. What is it that we are called to preserve, to keep from going bad or becoming contaminated? But Jesus also warns us that we can "lose our saltiness." What do you think Jesus meant by this? How can we lose our "saltiness," our ability to keep things from going bad? Give some examples of this.**

NOTE TO THE TEACHER! If time permits, explore this question: Jesus also says that if we lose our saltiness, our saltiness cannot be restored. What does Jesus mean here? Do you believe that once we lose our saltiness, we cannot be restored? Give some reasons for your answer.

Desired Result:
To make youth aware of the profound effects that the shows they watch have on them.
(Choose Option A or B.)

(Allow 10 minutes.)

CONNECT WITH LIFE

SENSITIVITY CHECK

A

SAY:

➤ We have the opportunity to watch literally thousands of programs on TV. With the advent of the satellite dish, we can watch more programs than ever before. From *Cops* to *Melrose Place* to *Home Improvement* to major league ball games, we have a lot of choices to make when we have time to watch television! That is where we must be diligent. Whether we like it or not, what we put into our heads has a profound impact on our spirits. Ever notice that a horror movie makes you feel scared? Or that a sad movie makes you cry?

Think of the difference in network television in the last 40 years. It has grown tremendously and is more graphic than ever. More murders, rapes, and crimes are depicted in such detail that the inevitable happens: we become callous and lose our sensitivity. We could very well end up losing our "saltiness," our God-given ability to preserve what is good and to prevent the contamination or spoiling of God's creation—including our minds and our souls.

NOTE TO THE TEACHER! Help your group members see that violence and destruction are portrayed as the most common response to problems on television. From the "private eye" who finally "gets his man" in a bloody shoot-out to the cartoon character who drops a huge rock on his or her pursuer or blows up another character, violence and destruction are often depicted as the solution or remedy to problems.

ASK:

➤ Do you think that crime is glorified on TV or in the movies? Do you think that crime is made to look normal in TV or in the movies?

➤ What seems to be the solution for most of the problems depicted in television programs?

➤ What message goes into our heads as we watch violent act after violent act? Does this message square with the message of Jesus Christ? Give reasons for your answer.

➤ Do you feel that we are less sensitive to violence on TV than people were thirty years ago? Why or why not?

➤ Do you think that TV may influence people to reenact what they see? Before you answer, think to yourself: Have you ever tried to copy something you saw on a television program? Have you ever repeated a joke or sang a song you heard on television? What kinds of people are most

likely to try to reenact what they see on television, especially in terms of violence or revenge? What might these persons be lacking in their lives that we of the Christian faith have in our lives? Be as specific as possible.

B SWITCH OR STAY?

two cardboard cards or index cards with "switch" printed on one side and "stay" on the other. ***(Allow 10 minutes.)***

Ask the youth to form two teams. Give each team a card that has the word printed "switch" on one side and the word "stay" on the other.

SAY:

➤**Both teams have a card labeled "SWITCH" on one side and "STAY" on the other. As I read a scenario, each team will have thirty seconds to decide if they will stay with the channel I have described and watch the program, or if they will switch to another channel to watch something else. Each team will show their choice by holding up the appropriate side of the card.**

Expect the teams to disagree from time to time. Ask each team to defend its choice of switching or staying, not just in terms of interest in the program but in terms of the value of the program to the persons watching it.

SCENARIOS:

- **The Playboy channel is normally scrambled. But tonight it is coming in clear.**
- **HBO is showing its *Best of Ice Hockey Fights.***
- ***Home Improvement***
- ***90210***
- ***Monday Night Football***
- ***X-Files***
- **You're having a few friends over and its late. Your parents have gone to bed. Do you watch *Murder Live?* Your parents said you couldn't.**
- ***The History of the Civil War***
- ***Eddie Murphy Live and Uncensored* (you may have to explain "uncensored")**
- ***America's Most Wanted***
- ***Cops***
- ***ER***

Desired Result:
To offer God thanks for the many good and positive influences of TV and to ask for the guidance and wisdom to make responsible choices.

paper and pencils
(Allow 10 minutes.)

CLOSING CONNECTION

PRAYERS

SAY:

- **Write down the name of what you think are the three "best" shows on television. You decide what "best" means to you, but keep in mind all that we have said about the positive and negative influences of television.**

- **We have talked about many shows and how we might make better choices in what we watch. We are now going to thank God for the creativity the writers and actors have been given. After I start the prayer I will invite each of you to name your favorite show. You have listed three so if anyone else says your favorite, you will have another show to choose from.**

PRAY:

> **Thank you, God, for the wonderful creative minds that are working on television. There are many shows on TV that aren't good for us. Yet there are some that are excellent. They entertain. They teach. Sometimes they make a good impression on us. Some of them are:** (begin going around the room naming "best"shows).
>
> **Thank you God for these and others we have missed. Help us be responsible in our choices and help us always lean on your strength and grace. In Jesus' name. Amen.**

When each group member has listed a program she or he thinks is "best," close with these words from Philippians 4:8:

> *Finally, beloved, whatever is true, whatever is honorable, whatever is just, whatever is pure, whatever is pleasing, whatever is commendable, if there is any excellence and if there is anything worthy of praise, think about these things.*

Read Me

THIS IS WHAT YOU NEED TO KNOW ABOUT THE TOPIC.

Youth spend a lot of time watching television. A youth ministry resource magazine has said that "American youth watch an average of 3.5 hours of TV daily —18,000 hours by the end of high school, compared to 13,000 hours in the classroom" (*YouthWorker* May/June 1997 p.19).

So What If They Watch?

Television is one of those phenomena in our culture about which no one feels neutral. Some people see all television as the work of the devil and even go so far as to junk their television sets and refuse to allow their children to watch television at all. At the other extreme are those whose television sets are turned on the first thing in the morning and off the very last thing at night. These people eat family meals in front of the television and have forgotten the joy of conversation because of the incessant blare of the "tube." Fortunately, most folks are at neither of these extremes, but most are still struggling to understand what television is and what it isn't, what it can do for youth and what it can't do, and what it does that is good and what it does that is bad.

Here's the beginning of a list of positive and negative characteristics of television. Can you add other characteristics to each list?

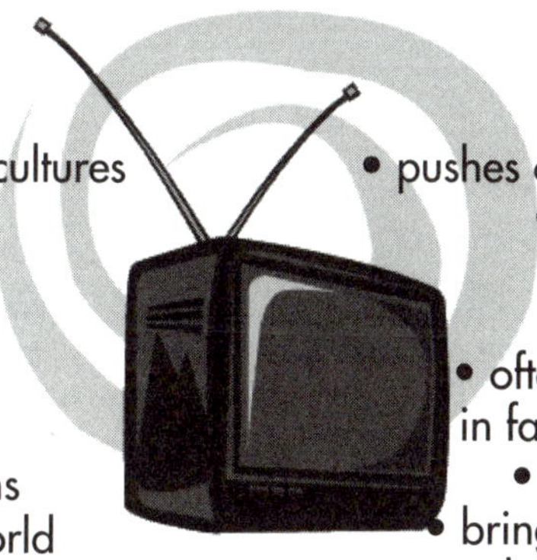

POSITIVE

- helps us learn about other cultures
- entertains
- inspires
- informs
- stimulates
- educates
- broadens our horizons
- keeps us up with the world

NEGATIVE

- pushes consumerism with constant commercials
- isolates us from one another
- glorifies violence
- overemphasizes sexuality
- often rejects marriage and the family in favor of promiscuous sexual activity
- portrays much of life as sordid
- brings to our homes those we would not otherwise invite into our living rooms
- belittles individuals and groups of people

Because of this mixture of both positive and negative influences, television must be part of our Christian stewardship. Put most simply, television is neither good nor bad, television simply is. It is our use or misuse of television that can be positive or negative, healthy or destructive, contributing to our life in Christ or detracting from our walk with Christ. The issue is not television, the issue is us.

WATCH AND LISTEN

Look at several different, popular television shows. Note the positives and negatives you see portrayed. Try counting violent scenes and sexual innuendoes. When you are done, are you surprised by the numbers?

Review the Scripture passages for this lesson: **Colossians 2:8; Genesis 1:31; Matthew 5:13.** Think about what you watched and how it relates to the passages that you will read when doing this lesson. Scripture speaks of "being in the world, but not of the world." Is that possible today?

Often we make judgment calls about the things that we see on TV. We can develop an "anything is OK" or an "everything is awful" mentality. Larry Poland, a Christian working to reach Hollywood for Christ, has said, "Most of the things we fear in pop culture are expressions of desperation. That's the hidden message" (*Group Magazine*, November/ December 1995, p. 24). If we can address the desperation and begin to look beyond the surface, we would find people in need of grace.

NIELSEN RATINGS

Here are some things to do this week related to watching television. Try them!

1. Keep a log of how much you watch television and what you watch.

2. Note if you are watching television alone or with others.
   - ➤ If with others, who—family, friends, or others?

3. Jot down the names of the programs (or videos) you watch.
   - ➤ Who chose what you would watch each time?
   - ➤ Who usually makes the choice of what you watch?
   - ➤ On what basis does this person (do you?) make that choice?

4. Pick a favorite time for watching television. Sit down and watch carefully, noting these things in both the programs and the commercials:
   - ➤ How many acts of violence did you see?
   - ➤ How many overt or subtle indications of sexual activity did you see?
   - ➤ How many words or jokes did you hear that you would probably not repeat to your minister or great grandmother?
   - ➤ Ultimately what was this program trying to do for you or to you? (Think in terms like entertain, teach, amuse, and excite.)
   - ➤ How did you feel after watching each program? Each commercial?
   - ➤ What changes do you want to make in your television viewing? Why?

If you are serious about making some positive changes, offer a silent prayer to God for strength and perseverance.

So TV Has Problems?

Perhaps after you finish your log for a week, you may feel that television has some major problems. Violence, sexual activity, total disrespect for others, selfishness—all of these are rampant on our television screens. So what can you do about it? After all, you are just one teenager out of millions of viewers of a particular show. But you can do something! Here's a list of things to try. Sure, they take time, but the results are more than worth your time, some first class postage stamps, and a few long-distance telephone calls!

- The moment you see something you find objectionable on your television, call the local television station immediately. Describe in detail what you saw, why you found it objectionable, and ask what the station will do about it.

- But be fair! When you see something positive, uplifting, educational, or really useful on television, telephone the local station immediately to thank them for putting the program on the air and to invite them to show more such programs.

- Who pays the bills for what goes on television? You're right: the companies that sponsor the shows. If you find a program objectionable, make a list of the sponsors of that program, especially those companies whose commercials have been shown several times during the program. Write to each of the advertisers (you may have to call the library to get addresses) and explain in detail what you found objectionable about the program. Include in your letter that you may find using their products difficult if they continue to sponsor such programs.

- But again, be fair! Write the sponsors of programs that you find positive and tell them you appreciate the contribution they are making through their programming.

- Want to go after the "big boys"? Do it! Write to the executives of major television networks: NBC, CBS, ABC, FOX, and so on. Again, get addresses from the library and address your letter to the "Programming Director." That may not be the exact title, but it will get you letter where it has to go. Let them know what you like and why or what you don't like and why! Your letter, your voice, your ideas do make a difference!

- Organize your family, your friends, and the others in your Sunday school class to write letters and to make telephone calls. Let your thoughts and feelings be made known. Television networks respond to the voices of their viewers.

Hint: Don't expect replies to your letters, but believe that they have been read and considered.

THE JOURNEY OF FAITH: WHAT CAN I BELIEVE?

SESSION 1: WHAT DO I PACK? PREPARING FOR THE JOURNEY

SESSION 2: WHERE DO I GO FROM HERE? ON THE ROAD

SESSION 3: HOW WILL I KNOW WHEN I GET THERE? THE TOOLS OF CHRISTIAN DECISION-MAKING

Purpose:

This unit will help youth clarify their Christian beliefs and the process by which this belief system is determined.

This Is Not Junk Mail!

IT'S IMPORTANT STUFF FROM YOUR TEENAGER'S SUNDAY MORNING LEADER

DOUBT AND BELIEF

As a person moves from childhood into adolescence, the process of defining a personal belief system begins to emerge. To this point, a young person has accepted the belief system of the important people in his or her life, such as parents, teachers, counselors, coaches, and others. But now the young person is beginning to form her or his own belief system through a kind of "trial and error" approach. That approach involves three stages:

- questioning
- exploring
- experimenting

And do you know what experimentation leads to? More questioning, more exploring, and the process begins all over again. Developing a personal belief system is a circular process of questioning, exploring, and experimenting over and over again. Make no mistake! Your teenager —and every teenager— is forming a personal belief system. For some teenagers, that system is rooted in the Christian faith, for others in the Jewish or Islamic faith. And for others that belief system has no roots in God or in any form of god, but instead is rooted in power, violence, money, acceptance by a particular group (like a gang or a clique), popularity, or any of many other sources of identity. Why is a personal belief system, the right personal belief system, so important? Because our perceptions of the world, of one another, and of ourselves are grounded in our personal belief system. We are talking here of something that will direct the life of your teenager from here on!

Keep in mind that faith—even Christian faith—is born out of doubt. Offer your youth opportunities to explore the sometimes abstract concepts of the Christian faith in an effort to develop a belief system rooted in God. Through this process, young people have a chance to become part of the story and to integrate their Christian faith into their everyday lives.

This unit will help your daughter or son clarify what she or he believes about the Christian faith, and it will also help him or her claim these beliefs for himself or herself.

TABLE TALK

Don't be afraid if your youth questions his or her Christian faith. Share with your youth times in your own life when you had doubts or struggled with making important decisions. Discuss the process you went through and describe the feelings that you experienced during that time. Relate how your faith was a part of the process. It is important for them to realize that you do not have all the answers and must rely on your faith for direction.

Perhaps you were at one time a member of another denomination or perhaps even a different religion. Talk with your teen about that experience. Describe those factors that led you in your own spiritual journey to the place where you are now.

Don't be alarmed if your teenager shows very serious interest in other denominations or other religions. This is a time of questioning, exploring, and experimenting. Some youth even go through a period of rebellion in which they reject the faith of their parents and strike out on their own, visiting other churches and reading about other religions. This is a normal process; it's a part of the journey. (Of course, be on the lookout for cult activity or for exclusive or over-commitment to one friend or a small group of friends.) But on the whole, a part of the journey is straying off onto side roads from time to time in order to better define the main path.

Be honest. You've been there, done that, and perhaps have a few scars to show for it. Don't be afraid to share these with your teen. The faith of both of you will grow, and the relationship between you will blossom.

Hallelujah!

IDEAS FOR PEOPLE WHO PLAN WORSHIP

The following ideas can be used for times of worship or celebration during your class sessions. You may also share these suggestions with your pastor, choir director, and worship chairperson to help them discover ideas and resources for making worship more youth-friendly.

SONGS ABOUT DOUBT AND BELIEF

Check your congregation's hymnal for these hymns or others relating to doubt and belief:

"Seek Ye First"
"Hymn of Promise"

You might also use two Amy Grant songs from *Songs From the Loft:*

"Where Do I Go"
"We Believe in God"

SCRIPTURE SUGGESTIONS

Matthew 6:25-34 (especially verse 33)
Matthew 22:36-40
John 3:16
Psalm 119:105

AFFIRMATION OF FAITH

The Apostles' Creed

SERMON AND MEDITATION IDEA STARTERS

We sometimes don't know which way we should go or what direction to take when making a decision. In the movie *The Wizard of Oz* Dorothy encounters Scarecrow at a crossroad in the yellow brick road and asks, "Which way should I go?" Scarecrow responds as he crosses his arms, "Some people go this way. Some people go that way. I guess you could go in any direction."

A rock and roll song from the 1970's was entitled, "Life Is a Highway" by Tom Cochran. Using the title of this song, a sermon could be developed on the different paths that a life of faith might take.

In a similar manner, one could also use the poem "The Road Not Taken" by Robert Frost to develop the theme of decisions and choices in life.

Miscellany

IDEAS FOR TEACHERS

When All Youth Are in One Class

Since the purpose of this unit is to talk about faith as a journey, keep in mind that different people will be at different points along the journey. Remember that younger youth learn more concretely, while older youth are capable of dealing with more abstract concepts.

As you select the activities for this unit, think about the particular students in your class. Create a safe environment where they can share their concerns and doubts while also challenging them to discover their own personal beliefs. Be sensitive to the needs of each individual. Know that some young people are easily intimidated in a group setting. Do not put your youth on the spot by asking someone to read aloud or share in front of the entire group if that is a challenge for that particular person.

This unit will be a great opportunity to encourage older youth to show younger youth that the faith journey is a process of growth. If older youth take their leadership role seriously, they can have great influence on the younger youth by sharing experiences that have helped them grow and mature in their faith.

Ground Rules

Consider setting some "ground rules" for this unit and ask all the youth to agree to them. Here are some sample ground rules; ask the youth to add to this list:

- No one laughs or makes fun of someone else's understanding of faith and belief.
- Everyone recognizes that some folks know more Bible stories than others, but that does not make them better Christians than anyone else. Christianity is a dimension of who we are, not what or how much we know.
- Everything shared in these sessions is confidential. That means we don't discuss what someone else said about her or his journey in faith with anyone! Breaking that confidence is a very serious offense.
- We are a community, and we believe that a community exists to help its members grow. A community is a group of people who support one another, encourage one another, care about one another, and pray for one another.
- In our discussions of the journey in faith, age does not matter. We remember that God called very young persons like Samuel and the boy whose lunch Jesus shared with five thousand; very old persons like Abraham and Zechariah; and teenagers like Jeremiah and Timothy. The high school youth in our group have much to learn from the junior highs, and the junior highs have much to learn from the high schoolers.
- We all learn in different ways. Some of us learn through music, others through reading and writing, still others in small groups, others alone, others by "seeing" things, and still others by "doing." Since no one way of learning is better than another, we should honor each group member's particular style of learning.
- We may not yet fully understand our Christian faith. But we are journeying together toward becoming disciples of Jesus Christ. In order to do that, we need one another's prayers and encouragement.
- Journeying together in faith is fun! We laugh together, but not at one another; we cry together, but never alone; and we celebrate together, embracing everyone in that celebration.

SESSION 1:

WHAT DO I PACK? PREPARING FOR THE JOURNEY OF FAITH

FOCUS

Before we can know where we are going on the journey of faith, we must identify where we are.

SCRIPTURE

Matthew 6:25-34 (especially verse 33)

HERE'S THE PLAN DO IT YOUR WAY

OPTIONS	TIME (minutes)	PREPARATION	SUPPLIES
INITIAL CONNECTION			
A Silly Trip Name Game	3-5		
B Road Map Hunt	5-7	obtain several identical road maps (or maps of the same place)	road maps (one for every 3-5 persons), pencils or markers
C If I Could Go Anywhere...	10-12		paper, pencils
CONNECT WITH THE SESSION			
A Don't Leave Home Without It	10-12	make copies of YouthPage	YouthPage, pencils
B Fire! Fire!	12-15	make copies of YouthPage	YouthPage, pencils
C Suitcase Collage	15-17	draw a picture of a suitcase on a large sheet of paper or posterboard for each youth; gather collage supplies	magazines, large sheet of paper or posterboard, glue, scissors; markers
CONNECT WITH THE BIBLE AND THE FAITH COMMUNITY			
A A New Perspective	5-7		Bibles, lists from previous activity
B The Bible Speaks to Me	5-7		Bibles
CLOSING CONNECTION			
A Packing for the Journey of Faith	3-5		
B Pray Together	2-3		

INITIAL CONNECTION

A SILLY TRIP NAME GAME

Desired Result: To introduce the concept of being on a journey.

(Allow 3-5 minutes.)

Ask the youth to sit in a circle. Ask for a volunteer to be the "starter." Tell the group that the starter will say the phrase, **"My name is ______________ . I'm going on a trip, and for my trip I'm packing ________________."** The starter should select an item that begins with the same letter as her or his last name. The person to the starter's left goes next, repeating what the starter said, then saying his or her own name and the item he or she will pack that begins with the first letter of his or her last name. Continue around the circle until everyone has said his or her name and added to the "packing list."

SAY:

➤ **Everyone has taken a trip of some sort. Some items almost all of us would be sure to pack for a trip while other items are unique to each individual. Today's lesson examines faith as a type of journey.**

B ROAD MAP HUNT

road maps (one for every 3-5 persons), pencils or markers
(Allow 5-7 minutes.)

Before class, gather identical road maps (or maps of the same area) and come up with a list of places to be located on the maps. Have youth form groups of three to five people. Each group will locate on the map the sites you have selected. After five minutes, call time and check the progress of each group.

SAY:

➤ **Everyone has been on a trip. Some trips are short whereas others are more lengthy. Today's lesson looks at faith as a trip or journey. Just as you have used a map to help you find the places that you want to go, we also need something to guide us in our journey of faith.**

C IF I COULD GO ANYWHERE...

paper, pencils
(Allow 10-12 minutes.)

Divide youth into teams. Each team should come up with a description of "the ideal trip." You might ask them questions like:

➤ **Where would you go?**
➤ **What would you pack?**
➤ **How would you get there?**
➤ **Who would go with you?**

Have each team record its answers and report its ideas to the group.

SAY:

➤ **Everyone has been on a trip, and most of us have dreamed about a place that we would love to visit. Today's lesson examines faith as a trip or journey.**

CONNECT WITH THE SESSION

Desired Result: To identify basic individual values.

A DON'T LEAVE HOME WITHOUT IT

YouthPage; pencils; chalkboard and chalk or a large sheet of paper and markers
(Allow 10-12 minutes.)

SAY:

➤ **Remember the slogan for a well-known credit card, "Don't leave home without it?" What do you think this saying means?**

Using the YouthPage, have each youth list at least five things they would never leave home without if they were going on a long trip. Have each youth share two items from his or her list with the group.

ASK:

➤ **What's a belief (about God, Jesus, church, and so forth) you would never leave home without?** (In other words, what's one of your core statements of faith?)

Ask each person to share his or her beliefs with the group and to describe why that particular belief is so important to him or her. Ask him or her the source of that belief, perhaps in a question like, "How did you come to accept that belief and to hold on to it so firmly? How does hanging on to this belief make you feel (secure, confident, hopeful, inspired)?"

As group members describe their essential beliefs, make a list of these on the chalkboard or newsprint. Does the group see duplications or similarities? If time permits, distribute copies of the Apostles' Creed. (See the YouthPage for the next session, page 74.). Ask the group to read this creed aloud and compare the contents of this creed with the list of essential beliefs they made.

B FIRE! FIRE!

YouthPage, pencils
(Allow 12-15 minutes.)

Using the YouthPage, have each youth list ten items that they would rescue and carry to safety if his or her house was on fire. (Assume that reality is not a factor and that the size of the object doesn't matter.) After each person has listed ten items, have the youth pair off and come up with a combined list of the five most important items. Have each pair read their list to the group.

ASK:

➤ **How was this exercise easy or hard to do? Why or why not?**

➤ **Why are these items important to you?**

Tell the group that you are going to "switch gears" a bit.

ASK:

➤ **What's a belief (about God, Jesus, church, and so forth) that is very important to you?**

As each individual tells the group his or her belief, ask him or her to describe the source of that belief. Perhaps a question like, "When and how did you come to believe this?" might help. As individuals share, make a list of these "very important beliefs" on a large sheet of paper or chalkboard. If time permits, distribute copies of the Apostles' Creed. (See the YouthPage for the next session, page 74.) Ask the group to read this creed aloud and compare the contents of this creed with the list of essential beliefs they have made.

SUITCASE COLLAGE

magazines, large sheets of paper or posterboard, glue, scissors; markers; YouthPage (optional) ***(Allow 15-17 minutes.)***

Before class, draw a picture of a large suitcase on a large sheet of paper or posterboard for each person in the group. Have each youth cut out pictures and words from magazines depicting things that are important to them and glue the pictures onto the paper or posterboard to create a "suitcase collage." Have each youth share three or four items from her or his collage.

ASK:

➤ **Why are these items important to you?**

SAY:

➤ **We are like this collage, made up of all of our experiences, beliefs, ideas, likes, and dislikes. We take these with us wherever we go, like taking a suitcase on a trip.**

ASK:

➤ **What's one belief that is very important to you?**

As a group member identifies an important belief, jot this belief on the chalkboard or a large sheet of paper. When all have cited one very important belief (or more), ask the group to try to cluster them into categories like beliefs about God, about Jesus, about the church, about prayer, and so on.
If time permits, distribute copies of the Apostles' Creed. (See the YouthPage for the next session, page 74.). Ask the group to read this creed aloud and compare the contents of this creed with the list of essential beliefs they have made.

Desired Result:
To introduce the Bible as a source of guidance for our lives.

CONNECT WITH THE BIBLE AND THE FAITH COMMUNITY

A NEW PERSPECTIVE

Bibles, lists from previous activity
(Allow 5-7 minutes.)

SAY:

➤ **Christians believe that God offers guidance for the journey of faith much like a road map offers guidance for a road trip.**

As a group, look up Matthew 6:25-34. In today's session, have individuals look back over their lists from previous activities.

ASK:

➤ **How might your lists change in light of this Scripture passage?**

➤ **What additional beliefs would you add, based on your reading and understanding of Matthew 6:25-34?**

THE BIBLE SPEAKS TO ME

Bibles
(Allow 5-7 minutes.)

SAY:

➤ **Christians believe that God offers guidance for the journey of faith much like a road map offers guidance for a road trip.**

As a group, look up Matthew 6:25-34. Have each person choose a specific verse from this passage that he or she believes offers needed guidance. Have each person tell the group which verse he or she chose and why.

Help group members understand that "guidance" comes from a need, a situation, or an experience. Ask for volunteers to talk about times when they have been anxious, times when they have worried about tomorrow, times when they have been concerned about the future. Do not press everyone to share; some group members may have experienced crises that they do not wish to discuss.

ASK:

➤ **What do these particular verses from the Sermon on the Mount say about anxiety, fear, and concern?**

CLOSING CONNECTION

A PACKING FOR THE JOURNEY OF FAITH

Desired Result: To acknowledge our need for God's guidance.

(Allow 3-5 minutes.)

If you used the "Silly Trip Name Game," close with a time of sharing when each person responds to the statement, **"I'm going on a journey of faith, and I need to ask God for help with ____________________."**

Remind your youth of their pledge of confidentiality, especially as persons share those areas of faith in which they need God's help. If time permits, ask your group members to consider this sentence stem silently, then share responses with the whole group: **Our church is going on a journey of faith, and we as a church need to ask God for help with ________________.**

Close with a prayer asking for God to hear each prayer request.

B PRAY TOGETHER

(Allow 2-3 minutes.)

Ask the youth to form a circle and join hands. Lead them in a time of prayer, asking God's guidance as each person continues her or his journey in faith. Pray for each class member aloud and by name. You might suggest that the people on either side of the youth for whom you are praying gently squeeze that youth's hands as you pray for her or him. Do not be afraid to make reference in your prayer to some of the individual concerns raised during the session. Include yourself in your prayer; ask God's guidance as you continue to lead this group of youth in their journey of faith.

Read Me

THIS IS WHAT YOU NEED TO KNOW ABOUT THE TOPIC.

KEY IDEAS

Each of us has a belief system; no one can function without some sort of belief system. We view the world, determine what is of value, and order our lives through the lenses of these beliefs. Many people help shape our belief system; persons such as parents, siblings, extended family members, teachers, coaches, friends, activity leaders, and even television personalities influence and shape what we believe. How does your faith in God fit into your belief system?

One of our opportunities is to help younger youth learn to recognize how family, friends, experiences, and choices shape and influence their emerging faith. Beginning to make these links is a crucial first step in building a mature and growing faith.

SCRIPTURAL BACKGROUND

The Scripture passage for the session (Matthew 6:25-34) is part of Jesus' Sermon on the Mount. Jesus' original listeners had much about to which to worry. They lived in a time of oppression and poverty. In addition, the religious institutions had become oppressive, dictating a long list of requirements for faithful believers to observe. Jesus offered a message of freedom and hope. He encouraged his listeners to rid themselves of their anxieties about life and rely on the strength and power of God to provide for all of their needs. This message of freedom and hope are just as relevant and liberating for us as it was for those listening to Jesus on the Mount.

TEACHER SUGGESTIONS

Involve each student as early in the session as possible. Youth need to be involved and to feel that they belong. Be aware, however, that some youth crave attention in whatever form they can get it; some youth might put forth absurd responses simply to see how you and their peers will react. Accept all responses; however, push youth to look seriously at what they believe.

PRAYER

O Lord, you have called me to help shape the faith, the belief systems, of the youth in this class. Each of these young people is precious; each of these youth is searching; each of these teens is a child of yours. Help me find the patience, the commitment, the sensitivity, and the faith to walk the journey of faith with these young people and to lead them toward you. Lord, I need your help. In Christ's name I pray. Amen.

GO AHEAD AND Groan!

It's OK to groan. You may be thinking, "Why do we have to do this faith stuff again? We did that when I was a little kid in Sunday school. Besides, what does it all have to do with life anyway?"

We do this "faith stuff" again and again because each one of us grows and changes. We are different people than we were ten years ago, last year, last month, or even yesterday! For example, remember when you were four or five years old? Even then you had a belief system—there were certain things that you believed and trusted and lived your life by. You believed in Santa Claus and the Easter Bunny. You believed in fairies and goblins. You believed that you'd get your wish—whatever it was—if you blew out all the candles on your birthday cake. You believed that someday you'd be a great athlete or movie star or president. You believed that your parent was the wisest person in the whole world and that your parent knew everything there was to know. You believed in lots of stuff, didn't you?

Want to believe in that same stuff, now almost ten years later? If you're like most young teens, your beliefs have changed tremendously. In fact, you now wonder how you could have ever believed some of the stuff you believed as a four-year-old. But in another ten years, you are going to wonder how you could have ever believed some of the stuff you believe now! You see, as you grow and mature, your beliefs change and take on different form and shape.

So what's so important about a set of beliefs anyway? Put simply, beliefs, your belief system (and everyone has one, whether or not he or she admits it!) helps you

- make everyday decisions
- choose your friends
- make major decisions
- determine right from wrong
- plan your future
- develop relationships
- reach your goals

Are there others you would add?

The big question, then, is where does our belief system come from? Does it come from the crowd at school, our parents, or from the television programs we watch? Or does it come from our faith in a God who loves us and cares for us? How we act depends on what we believe. If we believe in a God who loves us and cares for us, we are going to live our lives in one way. If we believe in getting ahead regardless of the cost, we'll act in another way.

What we believe determines how we live. What you believe right now determines how you live right now!

YOUTHPAGE

What would you grab from your house if it were on fire? Use the space below to list the things that you would save.

Don't Leave Home Without it!

Going on a trip? Here's your credit card. Now, what else are you going to be sure to pack for your trip? What don't you want to leave home without? Clothes, sure; toothbrush, certainly; comb, absolutely. But what else? Think now: What has God given you that you would want to take with you where ever you go? List those things below on the credit card.

SESSION 2:
WHERE DO I GO FROM HERE? ON THE ROAD

FOCUS

It is important to put beliefs into words; only then can faith be an integral part of everyday life.

SCRIPTURE

Matthew 22:36-40; John 3:16

HERE'S THE PLAN | **DO IT YOUR WAY**

OPTIONS	TIME (minutes)	PREPARATION	SUPPLIES
INITIAL CONNECTION			
A Because I Say So	9-11		paper, pencils or markers
B Agree or Disagree?	8-10	make copies of YouthPage	Youth Page, pencils
CONNECT WITH THE SESSION			
A A Creed for Today	12-15	make copies of YouthPage	Youth Page, pencils
B A Creed of Movement	5-7	make copies of YouthPage	Youth Page
C This I Believe	10-12	make copies of YouthPage	Youth Page, pencils
CONNECT WITH THE BIBLE AND THE FAITH COMMUNITY			
A Jesus Says	4-6		Bibles
B What Would You Do?	10-15	make copies of YouthPage	Bibles, Youth Page
CONNECT WITH LIFE			
A God Loves Me	2-3		Bibles
CLOSING CONNECTION			
A Write It Down	4-6		index cards or paper, pencils
B Prayer Song	3-5	obtain a copy of the album, *Songs From the Loft*	CD or tape of Amy Grant's *Songs From the Loft*; tape or CD player

INITIAL CONNECTION

A BECAUSE I SAY SO

paper, pencils or markers
(Allow 9-11 minutes.)

Desired Result: To identify individual and shared beliefs.

Divide the youth into teams of two or three. Ask the teams to list as many pieces of advice that they have received from parents as they can remember (for example, "Don't talk to strangers"). After five to seven minutes, call "time" and have the teams read their lists to the group.

Come to a group consensus as to which statements the youth now claim for themselves. Which ones do they follow? Discuss the responses.

SAY:

➤ **Most people's belief systems begin with core beliefs that have been passed down from parents to children.**

B AGREE OR DISAGREE?

YouthPage, pencils
(Allow 8-10 minutes.)

Refer to "Agree or Disagree?" on the YouthPage. Have individuals look over the statements. Then ask them to circle the statements they think their parents believe to be true and place a star next to the statements they themselves believe to be true. Discuss their responses as a group.

Can the group members agree on a stance for each statement? That is, can all the group members agree or disagree with one or more of the statements?

SAY:

➤ **For most people, one's belief system begins with core beliefs that have been passed down from parents to children.**

CONNECT WITH THE SESSION

A A CREED FOR TODAY

Desired Result: To introduce the Apostles' Creed as the church's statement of faith.

YouthPage, pencils
(Allow 12-15 minutes.)

SAY:

➤ **Through the years the Christian church has tried to state what Christians believe in short, precise statements called creeds or affirmations of faith.**

Refer to the Apostles' Creed printed on the YouthPage. Read the Apostles' Creed aloud together. Anticipating questions about the phrase "holy catholic church," explain to your group members that the word "catholic," uncapitalized, simply means "universal." The word "Catholic," capitalized and often preceded by the word "Roman" (Roman Catholic Church), refers to a Christian denomination.

Divide the group into four teams (a team can be as few as two people). Ask each team to choose a part of the Apostles' Creed and to rewrite that part in the team's own words, using today's language. Ask teams to share their results with the whole group.

YouthPage
(Allow 5-7 minutes.)

B A CREED OF MOVEMENT

SAY:

➤ **Through the years the Christian church has tried to state what Christians believe in short, precise statements called creeds or affirmations of faith.**

Refer to the Apostles' Creed printed on the YouthPage. Assign one line or one section of the creed to an individual or team. Invite each individual or team to come up with a gesture, posture, or movement that suggests the assigned line or portion. When all are ready, have each person or team demonstrate the movement and teach the group how to do it. When all of the youth have finished their demonstrations, say and "act" the creed as a group.

Anticipate questions about the phrase "holy catholic church" by explaining to your group members that the word "catholic," uncapitalized, simply means "universal." The word "Catholic," capitalized and preceded by "Roman" (Roman Catholic Church), refers to a Christian denomination.

YouthPage, pencils
(Allow 10-12 minutes.)

C THIS I BELIEVE

SAY:

➤ **A creed is a statement of belief. The church has several creeds that it holds to be true. One such creed is called the Apostles' Creed.**

Call the group's attention to the Apostles' Creed printed on the YouthPage. Read the creed aloud as a group, then go through it phrase by phrase, discussing what each phrase means. Point out the three sections of the creed: the first dealing with God; the second dealing with Jesus Christ; the third dealing with the Holy Spirit, the church, forgiveness, and life everlasting. Anticipate questions about the phrase "holy catholic church" by explaining to your group members that the word "catholic," uncapitalized, simply means "universal." The word "Catholic," capitalized and preceded by "Roman" (Roman Catholic Church), refers to a Christian denomination.

Form small groups and ask each group to come up with a statement of belief concerning God the Father, God the Son, and God the Spirit (or the church, or the forgiveness of sin, or eternal life). Have each small group read their statements to the whole group.

CONNECT WITH THE BIBLE AND THE FAITH COMMUNITY

Desired Result:
To examine Scripture.

A JESUS SAYS

Bibles
(Allow 4-6 minutes.)

Tell the group that Jesus summarized his teachings several times during his earthly ministry and that one of those summaries is found in Matthew 22:36-40. (If your group enjoys Bible study, you might tell them that this same summary is found in slightly different words in Mark 12:28-31.)

DISCUSS:

- **How can we love God with our whole heart and soul and mind?**
- **What does Jesus mean when he says we are to love our neighbors as we love ourselves? How do we do that?**
- **What does Jesus mean by indicating that these two commandments sum up the entire Law, calling these the great commandments?**

ASK:

- **If we accepted Jesus' definition of the greatest commandments, how would our daily lives be affected?**
- **What things would we start doing and what might we stop doing?**

B WHAT WOULD YOU DO?

Bibles, YouthPage
(Allow 10-15 minutes.)

SAY:

- **Jesus summarized his teachings several times during his earthly ministry, and one of those summaries is found in Matthew 22:36-40.** (If your group enjoys Bible study, you might tell them that this same summary is found in slightly different words in Mark 12:28-31.)

DISCUSS:

- **How can we love God with our whole heart and soul and mind?**
- **What does Jesus mean when he says we are to love our neighbors as we love ourselves? How do we do that?**
- **What does Jesus mean by indicating that these two commandments are a summary of the entire Law, and that these are the great commandments?**

Divide the group into teams. Have each team develop and act out a roleplay concerning the effects of living out these two commandments in everyday life. Sample roleplays may be found on the YouthPage.

Allow time for performing the roleplays. As a group, discuss the various scenarios. Reread Matthew 22:26-30 aloud to remind the group of the central message of Jesus.

Desired Result:
To affirm God's willingness to be active in our lives.

Bible
(Allow 2-3 minutes.)

CONNECT WITH LIFE

GOD LOVES ME

SAY:

- **Another of the central messages of Jesus is summarized in John 3:16.**
- **What does this message mean?**
- **How does it affect your own life?**

Have the group read aloud this passage. Offer your own thoughts concerning the meaning of this verse.

Ask the group to form a circle. Have the group repeat the verse, inserting the name of each person in the group for the words "the world." (For example: "For God so loved ___________, that he gave his only Son...")

Desired Result:
To pray for God's guidance in helping us act out our beliefs in our daily lives.

index cards or paper, pencils
(Allow 4-6 minutes.)

CLOSING CONNECTION

A WRITE IT DOWN

Remind the group of the message of Matthew 22:36-40. Give each individual an index card. Ask each person to write on the card one way she or he will live out the message of Matthew 22:36-40 this week.

Suggest that each person to put his or her card in a pocket or purse, in a school notebook, or on a dresser at home so that it will be before him or her all week.

Close this session by asking the youth to stand in a circle and join hands while you pray aloud for each group member by name.

CD or tape of Amy Grant's ***Songs From the Loft;*** *tape or CD player*
(Allow 3-5 minutes.)

B PRAYER SONG

Invite the group to listen to the song "We Believe in God." Ask the youth to pray in silence for thirty seconds.

Close this session by asking the youth to stand in a circle and join hands while you pray aloud for each group member by name.

Read Me

THIS IS WHAT YOU NEED TO KNOW ABOUT THE TOPIC.

KEY IDEAS

Being able to articulate what you believe is crucial for putting your faith into action. Youth need opportunities to formulate statements of faith in loving and supportive groups. This is why being open to each student's attempts at stating beliefs is so crucial. Belittling, laughing, rejecting, or contradicting a youth's attempt at describing what she or he believes is destructive and cruel. Be sure your entire group is open to one another, that each respects every other member of the group, and that confidentiality is honored outside of the group sessions.

The church, through established creeds, offers a foundation upon which youth can build a belief system. While the church's formal creeds are helpful benchmarks and checklists, they may not be as relevant to a contemporary youth as the youth's own attempt to struggle with stating a belief.

Creeds and affirmations of faith are crucial starting places for understanding and for formulating our own living faith. But the church's traditional statements of faith should not be seen as the end of faith, for no creed or affirmation can say all about God, Christ, and the Holy Spirit that needs to be said. Nor can any creed describe for you—or for any teenager—what your relationship is with the living Christ.

SCRIPTURAL BACKGROUND

Jesus was raised as a faithful Jew. He knew the Torah and he followed its words. The first part of today's Scripture is the Old Testament *shema* (Deuteronomy 6:4), which places God at the center of life. Jesus adds a second commandment concerning love of one's neighbor. This passage contains the central message of the teachings of Jesus. In fact, a careful study of the words of Jesus in the Gospels will demonstrate that the majority of Jesus' teachings were devoted to helping people truly love God and genuinely love one another. Many of the conflicts Jesus had with some of the Pharisees were precisely over this issue: some of the Pharisees were so intent on following the details of the Law that they had forgotten its true purpose as a tool to help people love God and neighbor.

TEACHER SUGGESTIONS

This session uses the church's traditional creed, the Apostles' Creed. If your church uses another creed, you can substitute it for the Apostles' Creed. Before you teach, study the creed and become familiar with its words and concepts. For example, what does "born of the virgin Mary" mean and why is this significant? What does "resurrection of the body" mean? Feel free to consult with your pastor on these issues.

PRAYER

O Lord, help me this week to love you and to love the youth whom I seek to teach. Be with each of them as I pray for each by name. (PRAY FOR EACH MEMBER BY NAME, ADDING SOMETHING SPECIFIC FOR EACH YOUTH.) **Make my life an example and a worthy witness to your grace and love. In Christ's name. Amen.**

YOUTHPAGE

AGREE OR DISAGREE?

Which of these statements do you believe to be true? Circle the statements that you think your parents believe are true and put stars next to those you believe are true.

- Private schools offer better education than public schools.
- Girls are smarter than boys.
- A good education helps you land a good job.
- You are judged by the company you keep.
- Smoking is bad for one's health.
- You must be a friend in order to have friends.
- It is not what you know but who you know.
- Going to church helps you be a better person.
- God knows everything about me.
- Everyone tells a lie now and then; sometimes it's all right to tell a little lie if no one is hurt by it.

WHAT WOULD YOU DO?

- It is Sunday morning, and you are preparing to attend worship. You go to the breakfast table where your dad informs you that he has decided to play golf and will not be able to drive you to church. What might you do?
- The class nerd asks you to be his or her partner for a month-long project. You know that no one else wants to do it. What could you do?
- Your Sunday school teacher is really boring. Some of your friends decide to pull a mean prank on him and ask you to help out. What might you do?

A WORD FROM OUR SPONSOR:

MATTHEW 22:36-40

"Teacher, which commandment in the law is the greatest?" He said to him, " 'You shall love the Lord your God with all your heart, and with all your soul, and with all your mind.' This is the greatest and first commandment. And a second is like it: 'You shall love your neighbor as yourself.' On these two commandments hang all the law and the prophets."

Jesus offers guidance for our words and actions. How might these words affect your life this week?

THE APOSTLES' CREED

ECUMENICAL VERSION

I believe in God, the Father Almighty,
creator of heaven and earth;

I believe in Jesus Christ, his only Son, our Lord,
who was conceived by the Holy Spirit,
born of the Virgin Mary,
suffered under Pontius Pilate,
was crucified, died, and was buried;
he descended to the dead.
On the third day he rose again;
he ascended into heaven,
is seated at the right hand of the Father,
and will come again to judge the living and the dead.

I believe in the Holy Spirit,
the holy catholic church,
the communion of saints,
the forgiveness of sins,
the resurrection of the body,
and the life everlasting. Amen.

SESSION 3:

HOW WILL I KNOW WHEN I GET THERE? TOOLS OF CHRISTIAN DECISION-MAKING

FOCUS

The church provides a foundation upon which decisions can be made. These tools equip us to serve as disciples of Jesus Christ.

SCRIPTURE

Psalm 119:105

HERE'S THE PLAN DO IT YOUR WAY

OPTIONS	TIME (minutes)	PREPARATION	SUPPLIES
INITIAL CONNECTION			
A Today's Decisions	7-9		large sheet of paper and markers or chalkboard and chalk
B Decisions! Decisions!	6-8		paper; pencils; chalkboard and chalk or paper and markers
CONNECT WITH THE SESSION			
A Would You?	9-12	make copies of YouthPage	YouthPage
B Consequences	14-16	make copies of YouthPage	YouthPage, paper, pencils
C Stand or Sit	6-8	make copies of YouthPage	YouthPage
CONNECT WITH LIFE			
A Decision-making Tools	4-6	make copies of YouthPage	YouthPage
B Where Do We Get Our Tools?	4-6	make copies of YouthPage	YouthPage
CLOSING CONNECTION			
A Biblical Wisdom	2-3		Bibles, a large sheet of paper
B Teach a Song	3-4	make copies of YouthPage (optional)	Bibles, hymnals, YouthPage (optional)

Desired Result:
To recognize that we all make decisions daily.

a large sheet of paper and markers or chalkboard and chalk
(Allow 7-9 minutes.)

INITIAL CONNECTION

A TODAY'S DECISIONS

As a group, brainstorm all the decisions that have been made by you or for you today. For example:

- ➤ Who decided what time you would get up?
- ➤ Who decided what you would eat for breakfast?
- ➤ Who decided that you would come to Sunday school? to this class?
- ➤ Who decided how you would get here (walking, riding in a car)?
- ➤ Who decided what you would discuss once you arrived here?
- ➤ Who decided where you would sit in this class?
- ➤ Who decided who would sit next to you?

Use the chalkboard or a large sheet of paper to list in one column some of the decisions the youth made for themselves today, and jot down in a second column some of the decisions that were made for the class members by others today.

SAY:

➤ **Our lives are an endless series of decisions, some major, many minor. Yet each decision that we make for ourselves comes from our belief system, and each decision that is made for us comes from another's belief system. Figuring out how we make decisions is important because our decisions determine our futures and affect people around us. The most basic dimension of our faith is our decision to declare Jesus Christ as Lord of our lives. As growing disciples, we need to explore and clarify what we base our decisions on and why we make them.**

paper; pencils; chalkboard and chalk or a large sheet of paper and markers
(Allow 6-8 minutes.)

B DECISIONS! DECISIONS!

ASK:

➤ **List seven to ten decisions that have been made for you by others during the past week.** (For example, who decided what you would do in school or would have for supper?)

Ask the group members to quickly share some of these decisions with the group. Jot them down in one column on the chalkboard or a large sheet of paper.

Now ask each group member to list seven to ten decisions that he or she has made on his or her own during the past week (examples: what to eat for lunch; what tapes or CDs to listen to in his or her room; when and how to do homework assignments). Again, ask the youth to share some of these with the group and jot them down in a second column on the chalkboard or a large sheet of paper.

Look over both lists. Which ones are major decisions that have long-term ramifications? Which are relatively minor or insignificant decisions?

SAY:

➤ **We all make decisions. Some are conscious while others are unconscious.** (Give an example of a conscious and an unconscious decision from your own life.) **Figuring out how we make decisions is important because our decisions determine our futures and affect people around us.**

CONNECT WITH THE SESSION

Desired Result: To learn that each decision carries consequences.

A WOULD YOU?

YouthPage
(Allow 9-12 minutes.)

Refer to the YouthPage section entitled, "Would You...?" Go through each of the questions, allowing the youth to respond to each one. Discuss their answers.

ASK:

➤ **Why did you say yes or no?**

➤ **What influenced your decision?**

➤ **What might the consequences of your decision be?**

SAY:

➤ **Each decision has consequences. Being aware of the possible consequences before making a decision can aid you in making wise decisions.**

ASK:

➤ **How can you know the consequences of your decisions? Do you always know in advance the consequences of your decisions?**

➤ **How do you make decisions if you are unsure of the consequences?**

➤ **Does being a Christian influence your decisions? Why or why not?**

B CONSEQUENCES

YouthPage, paper, pencils
(Allow 14-16 minutes.)

Refer to the "Would You...?" section from the YouthPage. Choose one of the situations that most interests your group. Divide the group into smaller teams and assign one of the following responses to each team: yes or no. As a team, list all the possible consequences that might occur because of this response. Have the teams relate their lists of consequences to the whole group.

SAY:

➤ **Each decision has consequences. Being aware of the possible consequences before making a decision can aid you in making wise decisions.**

ASK:

➤ **How can you know the consequences of your decisions? Do you always know in advance the consequences of your decisions?**

➤ **How do you make decisions if you are unsure of the consequences?**

➤ **Does being a Christian influence your decisions? Why or why not?**

YouthPage
(Allow 6-8 minutes.)

STAND OR SIT

Refer to the YouthPage section entitled, "Would You...?" Have youth respond to each question by standing if their response is "yes" and sitting if their response is "no." Discuss responses. (Why did you say yes or no? What influenced your decision?)

Now ask the group members if any of them had difficulty either sitting or standing in response to some of the situations. Explore the reasons why they had difficulty. Discuss how the specifics of a situation may influence a decision.

ASK:

➤ **Would you let a friend cheat off your test?**

➤ **Given the following circumstances, would you respond differently and, if so, how would you respond?**

- **if the friend did not study because she or he was out cruising all night?**
- **if the friend did not study because he or she was taking care of a sick parent all night?**
- **if the friend did not study because she or he had to work all night to help with the household bills since her or his parent had lost his or her job?**
- **if the friend had just gotten over being very ill for two weeks, but the teacher was not willing to allow your friend to take a makeup test?**
- **if the friend had allowed you to look on her or his answer sheet during the last test?**

ASK:

➤ **What might the consequences of your decision be?**

SAY:

➤ **Each decision has consequences. Being aware of the possible consequences before making a decision can aid you in making wise decisions. How can you know the consequences of your decisions? Do you always know in advance the consequences of your decisions? How do you make decisions if you are unsure of the consequences?**

ASK:

➤ **Does being a Christian influence your decisions? Why or why not?**

CONNECT WITH LIFE

A DECISION-MAKING TOOLS

Desired Result: To help youth begin to discover and use decision-making tools.

YouthPage
(Allow 4-6 minutes.)

SAY:

➤ **Making decisions is not easy for anyone. Some decisions we make seem insignificant at the time, but prove to be major later. Other decisions about which we worry may prove to be minor in the long run. How do we make decisions?**

As a group, list on the chalkboard or a large sheet of paper some of the factors that must be considered before making a decision. If the group members have trouble getting started, "prime the pump" with suggestions like these:

- **What are the short- and long-term results of the decision?**
- **What effect does my decision have on other people?**
- **What does the Bible say is right or wrong in this situation?**

Come up with a list of at least six factors to consider when making a decision. Divide the group into three teams and ask each team to apply this list to a difficult decision-making issue. Ask a team member to come up with an issue, or suggest the following as an issue:

> **You have reason to believe that one of your oldest and closest friends is experimenting with marijuana. When you ask your friend, he or she shrugs off your question and denies using the drug. One evening you get a telephone call from your friend's parent asking if your friend is using drugs; the parent is worried and suspects that his or her teen is using drugs. What do you say to the parent?**

Ask each team to report on its discussions and on the way the team used the factors. Look over the list of "Decision-making Tools" on the YouthPage.

ASK:

➤ **What would you add or remove from this list?**

B WHERE DO WE GET OUR TOOLS?

YouthPage
(Allow 4-6 minutes.)

SAY:

➤ **Making decisions is not easy for anyone. Some decisions we make seem insignificant at the time, but prove to be major later. Other decisions about which we worry may prove to be minor in the long run. How do we make these decisions?**

Look over the list of decision-making tools on the YouthPage and talk as a group about some of the sources of decision-making tools.

DISCUSS:

- How does the Bible help us make decisions? Does the Bible give clear direction for all the decisions we face?
- How do our parents help us make decisions? Is our parents' advice always right for us?
- How can the experiences of other people be helpful when we face decisions?
- Are situations alike enough that we can depend on the experiences of others?

ASK:

- What would you add or remove from the list of decision-making tools on the YouthPage?

CLOSING CONNECTION

Desired Result: To affirm the importance of Scripture in decision-making.

A BIBLICAL WISDOM

Bibles, large sheet of paper
(Allow 2-3 minutes.)

Read Psalm 119:105. Share with your group members how the word of God has been a lamp unto your feet, a light unto your path. Describe some specific examples from your own life in which the Scriptures have spoken to you and for you in powerful ways.

Now ask the group members to stand, join hands, and pray silently that the Word of God might also come alive in their hearts and be for them a lamp, a light for life. Close this time of prayer by praying aloud for each member of the group by name.

B TEACH A SONG

Bibles, hymnals (optional)
(Allow 3-4 minutes.)

Find and read Psalm 119:105. Read or sing (if you or someone in the group knows the tune) the song, "Thy Word," from the YouthPage.

Finally, ask the group members to stand, join hands, and pray silently that the Word of God might come alive in their hearts and be for them a lamp, a light for life. Close this time of prayer by praying aloud for each member of the group by name.

Read Me

THIS IS WHAT YOU NEED TO KNOW ABOUT THE TOPIC.

KEY IDEAS

Youth need help in making faithful decisions, yet many youth lack the tools to make good decisions. They struggle with balancing short- and long-term results and consequences, the particularities of a situation, and the conflict of values: "Will this make me popular and liked, or unpopular and rejected?" Focus on decision-making tools in this session, sharing your own experiences as you do so.

SCRIPTURAL BACKGROUND

The author of Psalms is traditionally believed to be David, though most scholars today attribute the Psalms to various poets, whose lives spanned a long period of time.

Psalm 119, at 176 verses, is the longest psalm in the Bible. Each one of those verses praises God for the gift of God's word, the commandments, the Scriptures, the Law. Verse 105 is often memorized and quoted as a central theme of this psalm because it emphasizes the role of the Scriptures in all of life, including decision-making.

TEACHER SUGGESTIONS

One of the major concerns of teens is decision-making. Most teens are seeking the ways and means to make sound decisions. While some youth claim that they want no rules or boundaries, in reality, most do seek limits because these limits help them make wise decisions.

One of the most important factors in this session will be you, as the teacher, and your own willingness to share deeply of yourself and the ways in which you make decisions. The youth will look to you for the tools and the experience they need to make decisions. Do not be afraid to share of yourself, including your struggles and perhaps failures in making wise decisions. What you have learned and can share with them about the decision-making process will be of great value to them. Let them know you.

Also be up front with your students about the times that decisions are not clear-cut, when right and wrong, good and bad, better and worse, do not seem so clear. Sometimes decisions involve choosing between the proverbial "lesser of two evils," or making a choice that will help some people but hurt others. Decision-making is a complex process that leads us to both successes and failures. The popular bracelet, WWJD (What Would Jesus Do?), is a good guideline, but what Jesus would do in a particular situation is not always clear to everyone concerned. Two well-meaning and sincere Christians may come up with two different answers to what Jesus would do in a certain situation.

These are some of the reasons why letting your students know your own struggles with decision-making is so important. Let them know you, trust you, and love you.

Remember:

***YOU* are the most important curriculum resource in your class, especially in this area of decision-making.**

PRAYER

May the decisions I make this week be acceptable to you, O Lord. Prepare me to honestly examine the decision-making process with our youth. Amen.

WHAT WOULD YOU DO?

What would you do in the following situations?

- Would you be friends with someone who took your boyfriend or girlfriend?
- Would you let a friend cheat off your test?
- Would you give a friend lunch money if it meant that you would go without lunch?
- Would you still be friends with someone if your parents told you that you couldn't?
- Would you let someone drink from your soda can even if he or she had just gotten over the flu?
- Would you loan money to friends, even if they wouldn't tell you why they needed it?
- Would you continue to buy presents for a friend who never bought you one?
- Would you tell a very sensitive friend that he or she had bad breath?
- Would you remain friends with someone who constantly put down your other friends?
- Would you help a friend make a team event if it meant you wouldn't?

DECISION-MAKING TOOLS

Here is a brief list of some basic tools for making good decisions. As you read over this list, you will want to add other tools, perhaps tools that you have found useful as you have faced decisions in your life:

- The witness of the Bible
- The stories of Bible people
- The experiences of others whom you respect
- The counsel of family and friends who love you
- Insights from hymns
- Prayer, prayer, prayer!
- Time to consider consequences, time to consider the effect on others, time to consider the short- and long-term results
- The facts! All the facts, the true facts, the hard facts—not rumors or ideas or opinions or gossip, but facts!
- The experiences of persons throughout the history of the church
- Time to consider all the alternatives and options
- Conversation, discussion, honesty with those you respect—parents, teachers, pastors, Sunday school teachers, coaches, and other special adults in your life
- Prayer! Prayer! And more prayer!

Thy Word

Thy word is a lamp unto my feet
and a light unto my path.

When I feel afraid, think I've lost my way,
still you're there right beside me,
and nothing will I fear
as long as you are near.
Please be near me to the end.

Thy word is a lamp unto my feet
and a light unto my path.

Now I will not forget
your love for me and yet
my heart forever is wandering.

Jesus, be my guide
and hold me to your side,
and I will love you to the end.

WORDS: Amy Grant
MUSIC: Michael W. Smith

THE HOLY SPIRIT

SESSION 1: THE BREATH OF LIFE
SESSION 2: THE SUSTAINER, GUIDE, AND COMFORTER OF LIFE
SESSION 3: THE GIVER OF NEW LIFE

Purpose

This unit is designed to help middle school youth explore the presence and work of the Holy Spirit.

This Is Not Junk Mail!

IT'S IMPORTANT STUFF FROM YOUR TEENAGER'S SUNDAY MORNING LEADER

WHAT'S GOING ON IN THIS UNIT?

This three-session unit will study the nature and work of the Spirit of God. The first session looks at the Spirit of God as the giver of life, both physical and spiritual. The second session explores the work of the Holy Spirit, focusing on the Holy Spirit's presence in our lives to sustain and nourish our bodies and our souls, to guide us through the many decisions of life, and to comfort us in times of sorrow and distress. The third session examines the new life or spiritual rebirth that we are given through the Holy Spirit.

Very little of the teaching and learning is presented in lecture style, however. These sessions are packed full of experiments, crafts, games, fun, and exploration. But these experiences are not ends in themselves. They invariably end with the teacher making a spiritual point. Every session also involves a worship activity, from a "thanks" wind chime, to a breath prayer, to a poem based on "Roses are Red" to tell about new life in the Spirit. We hope your youth gains a strong sense of God's presence in his or her life and a desire to let God guide him or her through the many crucial decisions of life your youth are already beginning to face.

EXPLORE THE BIBLE WITH YOUR YOUTH

One way to strengthen and deepen the bond that exists between you and your son or daughter is to explore the Bible. Sometimes you can try this through simple discussion, but that won't work with some youth. If your "path" doesn't cross every day with your teen because of the circumstances of school and work, try these ideas:

1. Start a notebook where you both write down your questions or thoughts about a Bible passage.
2. You could also do the same with a tape recorder. This might be a unique and fun change of pace.

The Bible contains a huge number of references to the Spirit of God or the Holy Spirit. Many of those will be touched upon during these three weeks. However, some of the key Scriptures you may want to discuss or study with your son or daughter are:

- Ezekiel 37 (the Valley of Dry Bones comes to life through God's Spirit)
- John 3:1-17 (Jesus and Nicodemus: physical birth and spiritual birth)
- Acts 2:1-21 (The descent of the Holy Spirit at Pentecost)

Hallelujah!

IDEAS FOR PEOPLE WHO PLAN WORSHIP

HYMNS ABOUT THE *Holy Spirit*

Check your congregation's hymnal for these hymns or others relating to the Holy Spirit:

"O Spirit of the Living God"
"Spirit Song"
"Spirit of the Living God"
"Sweet, Sweet Spirit"
"Breathe on Me, Breath of God"
"Surely the Presence of the Lord"

A TRADITIONAL NATIVE AMERICAN PRAYER TO THE HOLY SPIRIT

O Great Spirit,
whose breath gives life to the world,
and whose voice is heard in the soft breeze:
We need your strength and wisdom.
Cause us to walk in beauty. Give us eyes
ever to behold the red and purple sunset.
Make us wise so that we may understand
what you have taught us.
Help us to learn the lessons you have hidden
in every leaf and rock.
Make us always ready to come to you
with clean hands and steady eyes,
so when life fades, like the fading sunset,
our spirits may come to you without shame. ***Amen.***
(#329 in the United Methodist Hymnal)

Holy God, We Praise Thy Name

WORDS: Ignaz Franz; trans. by Clarence Walworth
MUSIC: *Katholisches Gesangbuch*

GROSSER GOTT
78.78.77

A PENTECOST SERMON STARTER

Put the story of the Tower of Babel (Genesis 11:1-9) and the Pentecost story (Acts 2:1-13) side by side and compare the two. At Babel, God mixes up the language of the people because of their sin. Language differences create a barrier between people; sin does the same thing. Yet when the believers gathered in one place to worship God, God reversed the problem of language and helped them all come together as one. The tower of Babel was built to honor people; but the church would be built to honor God. The tower of Babel failed because of its sinful, self-centered mission; the church succeeds when it remembers that it does not exist to bring honor to people, but rather to God. The Tower of Babel story is about a great building that failed because of the sinful pride of its builders, whom God punished by creating language barriers between them. The birth of the church at Pentecost is about a great "building"—the church—resting on a holy foundation and resulting in diverse people overcoming their differences and working together for God.

A LITTLE HUMOR...

Here's a joke that might get the sermon above started off with either a giggle or a whimper, depending on how well you tell it!

A certain king on a tropical island received a wooden, hand-carved throne as a birthday gift from his subjects each year. Since the king lived in a grass hut, there was not room enough to keep his growing throne collection. The king attempted to solve the problem by ordering a second story built onto his grass home. Over the next several years, he stored his thrones on the second floor of his hut. Unfortunately, one day the whole upstairs collapsed under the weight of all those thrones, totally destroying his royal home. As he stood looking at the mess, one of his advisors commented, "Well, I guess you know the moral of the story, Your Highness. Those who live in grass houses shouldn't stow thrones."

Miscellany

IDEAS FOR TEACHERS

THE COMPETITIVE ADVANTAGE?

Some youth thrive on competition. Other youth do better if the class as a whole functions as a single team. Some youth are good losers, and some are not. You will need to judge whether or not it is appropriate to use a competitive activity with your class. If your class is composed of five boys who are all on the same basketball team and who love friendly competition, that is one thing. But it is an entirely different thing if your class has youth with a wide variety of physical ability and self-confidence.

If you do use competitions from time to time, vary the "playing field" of the competition. For example, some games call for competition at a physical or athletic level. Some teens will excel at this. Other competitions, like drawing the funniest cartoon, might be based on creativity or artistic ability. Some youth will shine in such a competition. Still other competitions can be of the more intellectual sort: "Let's see which team can be the first to locate six references to the Holy Spirit in the Book of Acts."

On some occasions, the teens that don't do as well athletically do quite well intellectually. If and when you do use competitive activities, vary the kinds of competitions and participate as teams, rather than individuals, as often as possible. Competitions are not inherently good or bad. They can create enthusiasm and excitement, but may also run the risk of creating bad feelings if handled poorly by teacher or by winners!

You can usually convert a competition to a non-competitive activity. Two or more teams doing anything (reading a Bible passage, running a relay race, pinning the tail on a donkey) may naturally compete to see which one can finish first. By contrast, as single team tends to create an environment where all pull together to complete a task. Keep in mind that competitions do not have to pit class members against one another. Competitions may involve challenging the group to beat the clock, meet a deadline, or some other "competitor."

One way to keep competition light-hearted is to include silly applause afterward. For instance, the winning team may get to take a silly bow while the losing team does a drum roll on the table. Or you might let the losing team invent their own ways of applauding the winners. If you wish to compete for prizes, it is usually a good idea to have enough prizes that the losers get a prize, too.

Life is competitive, and we need to learn to be gracious losers as well as winners. But the church represents the one place where we do not have to compete for love and acceptance. God bestows his love on us freely—we can neither earn nor lose that love by our actions. As Christians, we are called to love each other unconditionally just as God does. Competition, therefore, is certainly not a theme to play too loudly.

SESSION 1:

THE BREATH OF LIFE

FOCUS

The Holy Spirit creates physical and spiritual life.

SCRIPTURE

Ezekiel 37

HERE'S THE PLAN | DO IT YOUR WAY

OPTIONS	TIME (minutes)	PREPARATION	SUPPLIES
INITIAL CONNECTION			
A Cottonball-blowing Relay	10	gather supplies	cottonballs, straws, a variety of bubblegum, masking tape
B Build a Wind Tunnel	15	gather supplies	fan, strapping tape, cardboard box, sharp scissors, clear plastic or cellophane wrap, paper, fishing line, objects to test
CONNECT WITH THE SESSION			
A Bubblegum-Blowing Contest	10	gather supplies	bubblegum, an instant camera, cleaning supplies
B Displace Water in a Bottle	10	gather supplies; make a series of numbered marks on several two-liter bottles	plastic two-liter bottles; basin of water; straws or plastic tubing; waterproof marker
CONNECT WITH THE BIBLE AND THE FAITH COMMUNITY			
A Breath, Spirit, and Wind in Ezekiel 37	10	study Ezekiel 37; make copies of YouthPage	Bibles, pencils, YouthPage
CONNECT WITH LIFE			
A Breathing Awareness	3		
B How Many Times Do You Breathe in a Lifetime?	5	gather supplies	calculator, watch with second hand
CLOSING CONNECTIONS			
A "Thanks" Wind Chime	15-20	gather craft materials	bells or strips of metal, fishing line, wire coathangers, pliers
B "Breath" Prayer	2		

Desired Result:
To introduce the image of the Holy Spirit as wind.

INITIAL CONNECTION

A COTTONBALL-BLOWING RELAY

cottonballs, straws, a variety of bubblegum, masking tape
(Allow 10 minutes.)

Divide the class into two or more relay teams of 4-6 participants per team. (If you have fewer than eight students, use your judgment in forming smaller teams or do option "B" instead.) Give each team three cottonballs and each team member a straw. Use masking tape to designate a starting line and a finish line for the relay.

SAY:

➤ **Each participant must blow all three cottonballs like a herd of sheep across a designated line and back. The first team to have everyone complete this relay wins first choice at the pile of bubblegum.**

Make sure there is enough bubblegum for the losing team(s) to also have some. Be sure to read about competitive events on the "Miscellany" page for this unit (page 88). After the relay has been completed,

SAY:

➤ **The cottonballs have been "guided" like sheep by your breath. In the same way, the image of wind is often used by the Bible to represent God's Spirit guiding people through life.**

B BUILD A WIND TUNNEL

fan, strapping tape, cardboard box, sharp scissors, clear plastic or cellophane wrap, paper, fishing line, objects to test
(Allow 15 minutes.)

Have youth construct a wind tunnel from a cardboard box by cutting out a window for viewing in the side and covering the opening with clear plastic. On the two opposite sides, cut openings for the tunnel itself. Position a fan at one end so that it will blow air through the box.

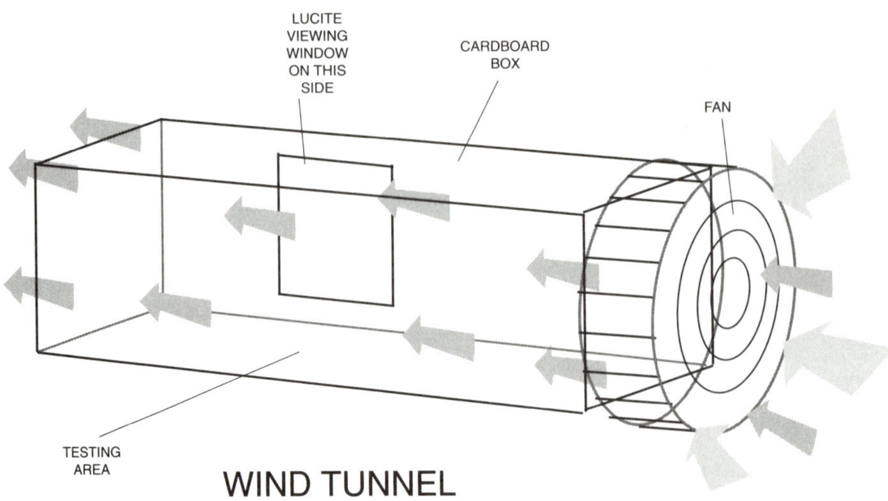

WIND TUNNEL

Gather various objects to place in the wind tunnel and have the youth guess how they will be affected before testing them. Try these or other items:

- paper airplanes (can youth make one that, attached at the front by fishing line, flies in a stable pattern in the wind tunnel?)
- house plants (how much will their leaves move when the fan is on low speed?)
- books (will they blow open or not?)
- a dish of whipped cream (will the cream fly off the top?)

Note the effects of wind on various objects and have fun in the process.

SAY:

➤ **In the Bible, the Spirit of God is often symbolized by wind. We cannot see the wind nor control it, yet we can feel its presence and see its powerful effect on our lives. This is also true of God, whom we cannot see but who is always present with us.**

CONNECT WITH THE SESSION

A BUBBLEGUM-BLOWING CONTEST

Desired Result:
To recognize the effects of wind.

bubblegum, an instant camera, cleaning supplies ***(Allow 10 minutes.)***

Bring a bag of various types of bubblegum. Allow youth to choose their favorite flavors or to mix different kinds of gum (within limits you set). Hold a bubblegum-blowing contest, using the suggestions below for possible competitions. The winner is the one who

- blows a bubble first after a signal is given
- blows one bubble inside another one
- blows two or more bubbles next to each other
- makes the loudest "popping" sound
- makes the funniest face or the funniest bubble
- blows the largest or strangest shaped bubble
- blows the bubble that lasts the longest (You might have to ask the students to remove the bubble from their mouth and observe during class—or declare a tie!)

HINT:
As a precaution, have cleaning supplies on hand, and give youth with long hair something to tie their hair back out of harm's way before the contest begins!

Throughout the contest, take photos and post them as memories of a fun time. Add a caption to the display like: "Just as we bring bubblegum to life, God breathes life into us," or "We thank you, God, for the breath of life."

one or more plastic two-liter bottles, a basin of water, straws or plastic tubing, water-proof marker
(Allow 10 minutes.)

B DISPLACE WATER IN A BOTTLE

Before the session, use a waterproof pen to make a series of numbered marks, in thermometer fashion, about a half inch apart all the way up the side of a two-liter pop bottle (you will want to remove the label first). Fill a small plastic or metal tub with water and place it on a surface that will not be damaged by any spilled water.

Give each youth who wishes to participate a straw. Have participants use the water in the tub to fill the bottle. Lift the bottle, bottom first, until most of the bottle is above water; but the mouth remains below the surface. This will cause the two-liter bottle to remain full of water. Then have the youth position one end of the straw underwater just below the submerged mouth of the bottle, take a deep breath, and blow air through the straw. The bubbles this creates will displace water inside the bottle and allow the youth to see a "measurement" of the amount of air expelled by that breath.

SAY:

➤ **Although we cannot usually see our breath or how much air we breathe, we know that we must have air to stay alive. God provides us with the air we need and fills our bodies with the life that comes from it just like you filled the bottle with air.**

CONNECT WITH THE BIBLE AND THE FAITH COMMUNITY

Bibles, YouthPage, pencils
(Allow 10 minutes.)

A BREATH, SPIRIT, AND WIND IN EZEKIEL 37

Have youth read Ezekiel 37 and ask them to underline the word "breath," bracket the word "wind," and circle the word "Spirit" each time these words appear.

ASK:

➤ **What is the difference between breath, wind, and spirit? In this Scripture, do they all represent the same thing or different things? Explain.** (Note: Different translations may use other words. Discuss the variations if it helps clarify the precise meaning of the three words *breath, wind*, and *spirit.*)

Ask each youth to answer the questions in the section, "The Breath of Life," on the YouthPage. After they have completed the questions, discuss their answers as a group.

Answer Key:
1—C; 2—A; 3—C; 4—E; 5—C

SAY:

➤ **The Bible teaches us clearly that God alone provides us with the breath of life, sustains us with the presence of the Spirit, and allows the winds of God's presence to blow through our lives and our world.**

CONNECT WITH LIFE

A BREATHING EXERCISE

Desired Result: To appreciate God's creative gift of life.

(Allow 3 minutes.)

Ask the youth to get comfortable, close their eyes, relax their minds and bodies, and focus on their breathing. Have them begin by taking a deep breath through their noses and slowly exhaling through their mouths. (You can tell them to try this technique anytime they feel tense, angry, or just want to relax.) Tell them you will give them a minute or two to breathe in this way.

While they are breathing, ask them to think about the gifts that God has given them and about how important it is just to have the gift of good air to breathe. Call time whenever you want to do so. Discussing the experience is optional, but you might want to point out that even though we do not usually think about our own breathing, it goes on day and night as a vital, basic gift from God.

B HOW MANY TIMES DO YOU BREATHE IN A LIFETIME?

calculator, watch with second hand
(Allow 5 minutes.)

Divide the class into pairs. Ask one person to count while the other person breathes. Explain that you will give everyone one minute to breathe normally. During that time, the person assigned to count should record how many breaths his or her partner takes during that minute.

Using the calculator, average the answers. Multiply the average number of breaths per minute times sixty minutes to find the average number of breaths per hour. Multiply this answer times twenty-four, and you will have the average number of breaths per day. Finally, multiply this number times 365 days in a year to get the average number of breaths in a year. This number, multiplied times 75 will give the average number of breaths a person might take during a lifetime.

SAY:

➤ **No matter what we do, we cannot increase the number of breaths that God gives us. Every breath that we take is a gift from God, just as our life itself is a gift.**

CLOSING CONNECTIONS

Desired Result:
To find an innovative way involving wind to thank God for the gift of life and the gift of the Holy Spirit.

A "THANKS" WIND CHIME

bells or strips of metal, fishing line, wire coat hangers, pliers
(Allow 15-20 minutes.)

Before the class session, shop at a craft store for metal tubes, small bells, or other items that might make good parts of a wind chime. Get a variety of items so the youth can be creative and make unique chimes.

Have the youth bend the coat hangers into a shape that suits them. Using fishing line, tie the "chimes" to the coat hanger. Let them temporarily hang the completed chimes outside your classroom or near a window. If that is not possible, hang the wind chimes in front of a rotating fan. After class, let the youth take their chimes home.

SAY:

➤ **When you hear the chimes, remember that, like the wind, the Spirit of God blows where and when it wants. Have you ever heard chimes clanging together during a wind storm? It sounds disconnected and violent. Are there times in your life when God's presence seems like clanging chimes in a blustery storm? We need to address the beauty of God's Spirit in our lives and the authentic experiences of God's Spirit troubling us in the midst of broken relationships, disappointing experiences of family, or personal conduct we regret and can't change.**

Close this session by praying together as a group. Ask the group members to stand in a circle. Invite the youth to take a deep breath and as they do so, to silently thank God for the presence of God with them, symbolized by the breath of God. Ask them to take a second deep breath and as each group member does so, ask her or him to pray silently for the person on her or his right. Ask for a third deep breath and this time offer a silent prayer for the person on his or her left. And ask for a final deep breath, this time asking each individual in the group to pray that the Spirit of God might blow across the class as it studies the Spirit of God in the weeks ahead.

B "BREATH" PRAYER

(Allow 2 minutes.)

SAY:

➤ **Prayers do not have to be "long-winded" to be meaningful. As we end in prayer, close your eyes, take a deep breath and hold it, and silently offer a "one breath" prayer. As you pray, gradually exhale until you are out of breath and, at that point, end your prayer. Your prayer may thank God for the gift of life, ask God for help with a problem, seek guidance for the coming week, or anything else you choose. The great thing about the "breath prayer" is that you can use it any time, especially when you need to relax or when you are in a hurry.**

Read Me

THIS IS WHAT YOU NEED TO KNOW ABOUT THE TOPIC.

THE TRINITY

One of the basic traditional teachings of Christianity concerns the Trinity. The doctrine of the Trinity talks about how there is only one God, but that God has three "persons" or ways of existing simultaneously. Traditionally, we have called these three "persons" the Father, the Son, and the Holy Spirit. Sometimes they are called the Creator, the Redeemer, and the Sustainer after their functions.

While the doctrine of the Trinity has always been difficult to comprehend and explain, one helpful analogy is to think of three drops of water, which, though distinct, are actually the same substance. Water may also have a solid form as ice or a gaseous form as steam. Whether water occurs (or "exists") in a liquid, solid, or gaseous state, it still has the same chemical composition and is the same substance. Similarly, God is still the one God, whether expressed in the person of the Creator of all things, or in Jesus Christ who walked among us, or in the continuing presence of the Holy Spirit.

HOW DO WE SEPARATE THE PARTS OF THE TRINITY?

When we think of their distinct functions, it may be that the distinctions we make have less to do with the actual "structure" of God and more to do with how it is helpful for us to understand God. For instance, it may be helpful to understand a football field in terms of yards, or in terms of its history, or in terms of the plays coaches design to be run on it. These are different ways to understand a football field, and yet they all speak of the same thing. Likewise, there are different ways to try to understand God, but it is important to remember that it is one God of whom we speak and whom we worship.

CREATOR, REDEEMER, SUSTAINER

When we think of their functions, the Creator makes things; the Redeemer saves us from our sins, and the Holy Spirit represents the continuing presence of God with us. What does God do in our midst? God comforts us when we grieve or feel afraid and alone. God guides our path in life and influences our direction. God sustains us by providing us with the gifts of food, clothing, shelter, loved ones, and so on. These are all important themes to stress for youth today. Jesus may have lived a long time ago, and God may have created the earth an even longer time ago, but God is still with us today through the presence of the Holy Spirit doing all the things God does—continually recreating, redeeming, and sustaining us.

THE GIFTS OF THE SPIRIT

In the New Testament, especially in the Book of Acts, the Holy Spirit is presented as a dynamic power that comes to those who accept the Gospel of Jesus Christ. This power enables them to do great things for God and to transform their own lives and the lives of others. But the Book of Acts also points out that the Holy Spirit does not make everyone act in exactly the same way. The Holy Spirit inspired Peter to great boldness; it inspired Barnabas to a life of quiet service. The Holy Spirit inspires some to become preachers and teachers; it inspires others to live out their faith in the midst of their daily lives. The Holy Spirit provides a great many gifts to those who trust God. Not everyone receives the same gifts, and we need to remember that no one gift is more valuable than any other. The greatest gift of all is simply that continuing presence of the Holy Spirit, God-with-us, in our lives.

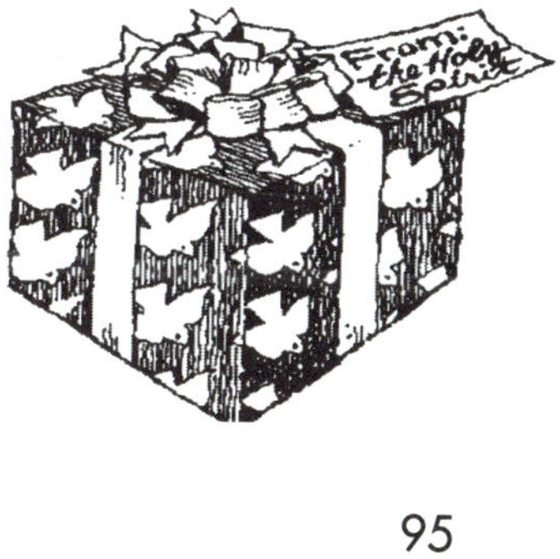

THE BREATH OF LIFE

The following questions are based on Ezekiel 37. If you have not done so, take a moment to read that chapter in the Bible. It's a little unusual, but interesting too! Just don't have any nightmares!

1. After reading this, I'd say that Ezekiel 37 is

   A. a true story that happened about 1500 B.C.
   B. the way that the Israelite people were invented by God;
   C. a vision that is intended to give a message;
   D. proof that Ezekiel was under a lot of stress and really needed a vacation

2. The message of Ezekiel 37 to those who hear or read this story is

   A. that living without God's Spirit is like death, but being filled with God's Spirit is life;
   B. if it were not for God, we would be nothing and have no mission in life;
   C. a body must have skin before it will hold air;
   D. none of the above.

3. Ezekiel's wife

   A. was home at this time and did not have the opportunity to visit the Valley of Dry Bones;
   B. was the third pile of dry bones to the left;
   C. is not mentioned in the story;
   D. was totally creeped out by the bones and wisely said "no way" when he asked, "Wanna go see a great place for a Halloween party?"

4. If you were an Israelite and heard this prophecy by Ezekiel, it should make you think that

   A. Ezekiel's wife was correct in answer D above;
   B. Ezekiel was saying that we have neglected God to the point that God's Spirit is not in us, and we are therefore no better off than a bunch of dry bones;
   C. we should change by seeking God's Spirit in our life and following it;
   D. we owe our life and identity as God's people to God's Spirit;
   E. all of the above except A.

5. The relationship between wind, breath, and spirit is

   A. the Spirit rides on the wind and avoids bad breath;
   B. the Spirit makes the wind blow, but not out of control like tornados and hurricanes;
   C. the Spirit, often symbolized by the wind, gives us the breath of life;
   D. the Spirit is symbolized by breath, and our breath creates small gusts of wind.

Illustration by Gustave Doré

ON 2:

E SUSTAINER, GUIDE, AND COMFORTER OF LIFE

FOCUS

The Spirit of God sustains us, guides us, and comforts us throughout life.

SCRIPTURE

Romans 8:26

HERE'S THE PLAN | DO IT YOUR WAY

OPTIONS	TIME (minutes)	PREPARATION	SUPPLIES
INITIAL CONNECTION			
A Scroll Hunt	5	prepare Scripture scrolls by printing Bible verses on 1/4 sheets of paper and rolling them up	paper and rubberbands for making scrolls
B Map Game	10		paper, pencils, candy bars
CONNECT WITH THE SESSION			
A Which Objects Will Float?	10	gather objects to test	bowl of water, variety of small objects to test
B An Ending to Sarah's Story	10	decide which version of "Sarah's Story" on the Read Me page to use	Read Me
CONNECT WITH THE BIBLE AND THE FAITH COMMUNITY			
Identify the Work of the Holy Spirit	15	read "About the Holy Spirit" on the Read Me page for Session 1 (p.95); make copies of YouthPage	Bibles, hymnals, large sheets of paper, markers, YouthPage
CONNECT WITH LIFE			
A Memorize a Comforting Bible Verse	15	gather materials	Bibles, chalkboard, scrolls from activity A in "Initial Connection" (optional)
B Puppet Show	15-20	gather supplies for making puppets	small paper bags or clean socks, items to decorate puppets
CLOSING CONNECTIONS			
A Holy Spirit Poster	5	gather supplies	posterboard, sticky notes, marker, pencils
B Self Hug	5		

INITIAL CONNECTION

A SCROLL HUNT

Desired Result:
To introduce the work of the Holy Spirit in a fun way.

paper and rubberbands or ribbons for making scrolls
(Allow 5 minutes.)

Before the session, prepare numerous "scrolls" by printing Bible verses on quarter sheets of paper, rolling them up, and fastening them with rubber-bands or ribbons.

Look through the Bible and select some of your favorite short passages, particularly those that give you comfort or provide guidance. You might use passages such as:

- Psalm 23, 51, 121, 139 (and lots of other Psalms)
- Proverbs (lots of them!)
- Isaiah 40:31; 43:1-2; 49:14-16; 61:1-3
- Lamentations 3:19-24
- John 8:12; 10:10b; 11:25-26; 15:4; 15:5; 15:9; 15:12

Hide the scrolls in an easily definable area that will not disturb other classes. For example, you might hide them in your classroom, the church kitchen, or the front yard of the church.

As class begins, tell the youth that the scrolls are hidden in the designated area and have the youth search for scrolls. Once all the scrolls have been found, have them unroll them and read the Scripture passage to the rest of the class.

SAY:

➤ **These are all good verses to tell us about the guiding, comforting presence of the Holy Spirit of God.**

B MAP GAME

paper, pencils, candy bars
(Allow 10 minutes.)

This game can be played indoors or outdoors. Divide the youth into at least two teams. Assign each team a different area inside (or outside) the church. Have each group hide a candy bar in that area, designate a starting point, and create a "treasure map" to guide the other team to the candy bar. For example, the map might say, "Start at the pump handle. Take three steps toward the white house. Turn right and walk fifteen steps. Take three baby steps toward the barn..."

Once each team has created a treasure map, have them exchange maps and follow the other team's map to find the hidden candy bar. After the hunt is over and the hidden candy bars have been found, you may want to reward all the participants with a candy bar.

SAY:

➤ **Like a map, the Holy Spirit is our guide in life, leading us to good things.**

CONNECT WITH THE SESSION

Desired Result: To understand that God is a potential source of comfort and help.

A WHICH OBJECTS WILL FLOAT?

bowl of water, a variety of small objects to test ***(Allow 10 minutes.)***

Pick out a variety of common objects for the class to test in class whether or not the objects will float. Make some obvious choices (ice cube, fishing bobber, rock, metal keys, drinking glass, scissors, staple, coin) and some not as obvious (fishing line, damp sponge, plastic toys, piece of scotch tape, sealed glass jar half full of marbles, feather, pamphlet, plastic push pin, ink pen, rubberband).

Place the objects on a table and number them. Have youth guess beforehand by numbering their paper and writing "float" or "sink" next to each number. Then do the experiment one item at a time; but before letting go, have the youth hold out a "thumbs up" if they wrote "float" or a "thumbs down" if they wrote "sink."

ASK:

➤ **What makes some items sink and others float?**

SAY:

➤ **The more buoyant an object is, the more it floats. In the same way, God's Spirit helps us become more buoyant and "rise above" the difficulties of life by guiding and comforting us.**

B AN ENDING TO SARAH'S STORY

Read Me ***(Allow 10 minutes.)***

Select and read aloud to the class one or more of the "How to Help Sarah?" stories on Read Me (page 104-105). Tell youth to invent an ending that they think would provide the greatest comfort to Sarah.

ASK:

➤ **Did Sarah made a mistake in each story? What should she have done instead?.**

➤ **What are her options at this point in the story? What advice does she need? And what advice would she likely get from the various people to whom she might turn for guidance?**

➤ **What possible Scripture verses might be helpful to Sarah to consider in her current situation?** (If you made scrolls, ask which scroll they think would be the most comforting to give Sarah.)

CONNECT WITH THE BIBLE AND THE FAITH COMMUNITY

IDENTIFY THE WORK OF THE HOLY SPIRIT

Desired Result: To identify the work of the Holy Spirit in Scriptures, songs, and creeds.

Bibles, hymnals, large sheets of paper, markers, YouthPage ***(Allow 15 minutes.)***

In preparation, read "About the Holy Spirit" on the Read Me page in the first lesson (page 95). Read portions aloud to your class or explain some of the main points about the Trinity and the various "works" of the Holy Spirit.

The goal is to create a list of things that the Holy Spirit does for us. Include in your study several of the church's creeds and hymns to see what they say about the Holy Spirit (a few are printed on this session's YouthPage).

ASK:

➤ **What did the Spirit do for the people in each of these Scriptures?**

- Psalm 51
- Isaiah 61:1-3
- Ezekiel 37
- Matthew 3:13-17
- John 3
- John 20:19-23
- Acts 2:1-21
- Acts 10:44-48
- Romans 8:1-11
- Revelation 2:7, 11, 17 and 29; 3:6, 13, 22

SAY:

➤ **From Genesis to Revelation, we see God's Spirit as conceiving and designing everything. But God's Spirit didn't stop after creating. In all these Scriptures we see that God holds together the world and sustains it even when we seek to destroy the world.**

➤ **God's Spirit is not remote and alien to us. The Spirit lives in us because God's love for us never ceases. The story of the Bible isn't just a history lesson. It's the living witness to God's Spirit giving on our behalf and living among us now.**

Invite questions from group members; expect some confusion as to the nature and function of the Holy Spirit. For example, some youth will liken the Holy Spirit to conscience; it is this, but much more. Others will think of the Holy Spirit as a warm feeling of excitement that comes over folks at some worship services; it is this, but much more. Still others will want to know how they can know if they "have" the Holy Spirit. Also, expect some questions about "speaking in tongues" and other "gifts" of the Holy Spirit. Be sure your youth understand that no single gift of the Holy Spirit is of more value than any other gift of the Holy Spirit. At least one youth is wondering if the Holy Spirit and the Holy Ghost are the same, especially if your church customarily sings the traditional Doxology during worship services. These are the same, "Ghost" simply being an older term not often used at present.

Desired Result:
To be reassured that the Holy Spirit of God is always present.

CONNECT WITH LIFE

A MEMORIZE A COMFORTING BIBLE VERSE

Bibles, chalkboard, scrolls from earlier activity (optional)
(Allow 15 minutes.)

Ask the class to choose a verse from those you have studied today (or a different one) to be their "Verse of Comfort." It should be a verse that they think they would find helpful if they need to be reminded of God's presence and power. The youth may select a verse that refers to the Holy Spirit, but do not "force" this. Let them choose their own comforting verse. Write the verse on the chalkboard. Say it aloud two or three times. Then erase a word and repeat it. Continue erasing a word or two before it is repeated each time. Soon it will all be erased, but the class will have memorized the verse.

ASK:

- **What does the verse mean?**
- **In what kinds of situations might the verse be especially appropriate, if memorized?**
- **What are additional ways you might want to keep the verse fresh in your memory?** (For example, they might write it on a slip of paper for their wallet, write it on a sticky note and put it on a their mirror, and so on.)

Before leaving this "comforting verse," ask each member of the group to turn to the person sitting next to her or him and to recite the verse from memory. Group members can help one another if the verse is not quite memorized by all.

B PUPPET SHOW

small paper bags or clean socks; items to decorate puppets (paint, colored markers, yarn, glue, etc.)
(Allow 15-20 minutes.)

Have the youth make puppets from small paper bags or socks, letting them decorate their creation using the paint, yarn, markers, or other materials you have supplied.

Divide the class into two small teams, if possible, and ask them to prepare a skit for the other team. Tell them to make up a situation similar to the ones Sarah experienced where a youth might need comfort or guidance. Using the puppets they have made, have the team members perform their skit for the other team. Ask the teams to try to include a Scripture verse in their skits.
If the youth enjoy this activity, one possibility would be to have that team perform its skit for other classes or perhaps the whole congregation.

CLOSING CONNECTIONS

A HOLY SPIRIT POSTER

Desired Result:
To celebrate the work of the Holy Spirit.

posterboard, sticky notes, marker, pencils
(Allow 5 minutes.)

Write "I believe in the Holy Spirit" at the top of a sheet of posterboard. Ask youth to write on a sticky note:

- one thing they have learned about the Holy Spirit during today's class,
- or one thing they appreciate about the Holy Spirit,
- or one thing they believe about the Holy Spirit.

When they have finished, have them stick their note to the poster. Put it up in the room for further reference, additions, and modifications during the rest of the study.

B "SELF HUG"

(Allow 5 minutes.)

Ask students to give themselves a "self hug." (Be cautious about telling youth to hug each other as part of a class exercise.)

ASK:

➤ **What does a hug mean to the person being hugged? to the person giving it?**

➤ **Does it make a person feel loved? protected? valued? close? trusted?**

➤ **What would a "God hug" mean?**

➤ **What would a "God hug" mean to a person who**
- **had just experienced a great loss?**
- **had just committed a terrible sin?**
- **was questioning if God even exists?**
- **cannot forgive another who wronged him or her?**
- **had just experienced a great victory or joy?**
- **was facing a very difficult decision?**
- **is in a great deal of trouble?**

➤ **And what would a God hug mean to a person who has no food? no home? no medicine? no job? no hope?**

The Holy Spirit speaks to all of these people in the particular way that each needs to hear. Ask your group members to think silently for a moment about how the Holy Spirit may be speaking to each of them.

SAY:

➤ **The continuing work of the Holy Spirit is a lot like a "God hug." The Holy Spirit lets us know that God accepts us, loves us, and wants to be close to us.**

Read Me

THIS IS WHAT YOU NEED TO KNOW ABOUT THE TOPIC.

This session includes an option called "An Ending for Sarah's Story." These scenarios allow the youth to imagine themselves in these situations, freely explore the options, and decide what a faithful response might be. Choose carefully whether you want to use one or more of the following stories. Be particularly thoughtful about whether to use the one about divorce with the youth that you will have in your class. It may be helpful for some youth to talk about their parent's divorce; other youth may be upset by the subject. The decision is up to you.

HOW WOULD YOU HELP SARAH?

In each of the stories below, Sarah has a problem and needs help or comfort. It is up to the youth to complete the story.

ASK:

➤ **To whom would Sarah most likely turn for help?**

➤ **What advice might she receive from that person?**

➤ **What would happen if she followed that advice?**

The characters that Sarah can turn to for help are:

- JENNY—Jenny is a close friend, but lots of times she does not know what to say or do. Sometimes she has given advice that is right on target, and other times her advice, if followed, would be catastrophic. But at least she is a loyal friend.
- MRS. PRESTON (JENNY'S MOTHER)—She is a busy psychologist and seems to have her act together, but Sarah has never had the chance to get to know her well because she is so busy.
- GOD—For the sake of this play, God will speak to Sarah through a beautiful angel.

STORIES ABOUT SARAH

1) One day Sarah went to a shopping mall. She happened to glance in a trash barrel and notice some money protruding from a crushed soft drink cup. She picked up the cup and discovered that it was stuffed with twenty- and hundred-dollar bills. Casually she slipped the cup into her purse and walked to her car. She transferred most of the cash into her purse, went back into the mall, and bought a whole new wardrobe and lots of new jewelry. On the way home she began to feel guilty for not turning the money in. She also feared she could be in danger if it happened to be drug money and someone had seen her take it. Suddenly she decided to take a left at the next light and go talk to...

2) Sarah was a star on her basketball team and helped them get to the state finals. Down by one point with three seconds left in the game, she drove toward the basket but was double-teamed. Sarah had always dreamed about going to the state finals and making the heroic last-second shot. One of her teammates was wide open under the basket. Unfortunately, it was the one person on the team who was jealous and never got along with Sarah; it was also the person who had missed a similar shot at the buzzer in the team's one loss of the season. In that split second, Sarah had to decide whether to pass the ball or keep it. She kept it, and her shot was batted away by the opposing players. After the heartbreaking loss, everyone on the team was strangely silent in the locker room after the coach tried unsuccessfully to

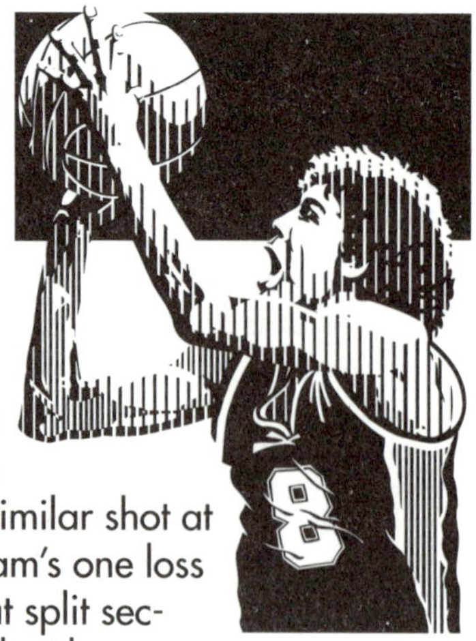

make them feel better. Then, in front of the whole team, the girl who had been open said sarcastically, "Way to go solo, Sarah! You ALMOST beat their whole team all by yourself!" Her remark really hurt, and Sarah felt like crying. Instead she...

3) One day when Sarah came downstairs for breakfast, her parents were standing in the kitchen. She could see they had been arguing again, but this time was different. Her mother was crying, and her dad had a suitcase. "I'm leaving," he told Sarah as he walked out the door. "I still love you, and I'll see you later. Meanwhile, you stay here with your mother." Then he left, shaking his head sadly. At first Sarah couldn't believe it. Then she burst into tears and ran upstairs to her room. Then she picked up the phone to call...

4) Sarah was walking home from school one Spring day when Megan, a girl in a couple of her classes, caught up with her and walked alongside her for a few steps. Sarah greeted her, but not warmly, as they were not good friends. Suddenly, Megan began to sob softly, and put her hand out to stop Sarah in her tracks. "Sarah," she said, "I need to talk to you. I know you go to church and all and read the Bible and all that stuff, so maybe you can help me." Sarah knew that Megan was not very popular. Her clothes were old and out of style, she did not live in the "nice" part of town, and she had a bad reputation in school. Still, she was weeping and asking Sarah for help. Sarah silently studied Megan's face while Megan continued: "I was out with a bunch of kids a couple of weekends ago, and we all drank some whiskey and smoked some marijuana. Other things happened and I'm afraid I'm pregnant. I know my stepfather will kill me! What am I going to do?" Sarah paused, then said...

After the youth discuss possible endings for these scenarios,

ASK:

- **Where in the world can God's Spirit be in each of these settings?**
- **Many times God's Spirit speaks and acts through disciples like each of us. In each case, what can be said or done to express God's love, protection, and care?**

YOUTHPAGE

WHO IS THE Holy Spirit?

Using a copy of your church's hymnal or songbook, copy portions from hymns, creeds, affirmations of faith, prayers, and other resources that tell you something about the Holy Spirit.

Here's a hint: Look in the "Topical Index" of your hymnal for a listing of hymns about the Holy Spirit. Read several of these hymns, even if they are new to you. Copy some of the words that you particularly like, but pay special attention to what the hymns say about the Holy Spirit.

Consider the following questions as you look for clues about the nature of the Holy Spirit:

1. **What are the characteristics of the Holy Spirit as described in these hymns?**

2. **What does the Holy Spirit do for us, according to these hymns?**

3. **Where does the Holy Spirit come from, and how do we know the Holy Spirit is with us, according to these hymns?**

4. **How do these hymns help you understand the Holy Spirit more completely?**

Hey! Copy this page for your youth—really, we want you to!

The Holy Spirit is...???

One of the greatest experiences of life is to receive compliments and encouragement from others such as:

> "Way to go!"
> "I knew you could do it!"
> "I love you."

After reading these hymns, creeds, and affirmations of faith, what can you say that's a positive statement about the Holy Spirit? Examples might be:

> "God's Spirit provides peace."
> "The Spirit sustains us when life's tough"
> "God's Spirit with me means I am never alone."
> "The Holy Spirit reminds me that God loves me."

Use the space below to list other statements about the Holy Spirit.

SESSION 3:

THE GIVER OF NEW LIFE

FOCUS

Jesus said that Christians are people who are born of water and of the Spirit.

SCRIPTURE

John 3:1-17, Acts 2:1-42

HERE'S THE PLAN **DO IT YOUR WAY**

OPTIONS	TIME (minutes)	PREPARATION	SUPPLIES
INITIAL CONNECTION			
A Signs of Life	10		a large sheet of paper, markers, paper, pencils
B Babble Language	10		paper, pencils
CONNECT WITH THE SESSION			
A Balloon Stomp	10	gather supplies	balloons, string
B Flip Booklet	20	gather supplies	paper, paper cutter or scissors, pencils, Bibles
CONNECT WITH THE BIBLE AND THE FAITH COMMUNITY			
A Jesus and Nicodemus	10	read "Nicodemus—The Rest of the Story" on Read Me (page 115); obtain several Bible dictionaries and concordances	Bibles, Bible dictionary, concordance, paper, pencils
B Crayon Picture Banner	10		Bibles, crayons, paper
CONNECT WITH LIFE			
A By Water and By Spirit	10		a large sheet of paper, markers, hymnals
B Zany Roundtable Discussion	15	invite and prep adult guests; make sure your hymnal contains the Apostles' Creed and the Nicene Creed	paper, markers, hymnals (or copies of the Apostles' Creed and Nicene Creed
CLOSING CONNECTIONS			
A Create a Rap, Song, or Poem	10		large sheet of paper, markers, Bibles
B Fill in the Blanks	5	make copies of the YouthPage	YouthPage, pencils

INITIAL CONNECTION

SIGNS OF LIFE

A

Desired Result:
To introduce the theme of new life through the Spirit.

large sheet of paper, markers, paper, pencils
(Allow 10 minutes.)

Divide the youth into teams of two. Tell them to pretend they are alien investigators from another planet looking for signs of life in this place. Explain that if your church were uninhabited, it would look a lot different than it does now. Have them walk around the building in teams and write down ten signs that show that the church is alive and active. Give them five minutes, and then reassemble as a group. Have several volunteers read their "signs of life."

Make a list on a large sheet of paper and post it for the rest of the class. Once you have the list,

ASK:

➤ **Which of these signs indicate that this is a religious place or that God is alive here too? If you were going to change the list to include signs of God's presence, what would you add so that the alien investigators would know that there are more than just people are here?**

BABBLE LANGUAGE

B

paper, pencils
(Allow 10 minutes.)

Have each youth write a short sentence on a piece of paper using simple words such as, "Hi! My name is ..." or "My dog's name is Fido." Then tell them that they are about to learn a new and exciting babble language. Now instruct the youth to rewrite the sentence adding the letters "ob" before each vowel sound. Therefore, "My dog's name is Fido" would then become: "Moby dobog's nobame obis Fobidobo." Once they have finished, ask everyone read their sentence aloud at the same time. Then go around the room and have each youth read their sentence for the class, letting the other youth guess what the original sentence was.

SAY:

➤ **In the Pentecost story, people spoke different languages and could not understand one another. But then the Holy Spirit came upon them, and they were able to understand each other. The Holy Spirit broke down the barriers between people and created the community of believers we call the church.**

Desired Result:
To illustrate the idea of new life.

CONNECT WITH THE SESSION

A BALLOON STOMP

balloons, string
(Allow 10 minutes.)

Give each youth a balloon to blow up and a piece of string several feet long. Have each person tie one end of the string around the balloon and the other end around his or her ankle. Designate boundaries around a specific, small area. At your signal, the youth should attempt to stomp on other people's balloons while trying to keep their own intact. Tell them that when their balloon is broken, they can replace it with a new one. When the game is over,

SAY:

➤ **Usually you are considered "out" when your balloon has been burst. But when you received a new balloon you were given a second chance, a new life. That is one of the things the Holy Spirit does for us—gives us new life. That's what we will be focusing on today. Christians are people who are born of water or baptized, and "born again" or given a new spiritual birth through the Holy Spirit.**

B FLIP BOOKLET.

paper, paper cutter or scissors, pencils, Bibles
(Allow 20 minutes.)

Have youth cut at least 15-20 small pieces of paper exactly the same size (approximately 3″ tall and 5″ wide) and put them in a stack. Ask them to draw stick figures to create a moving picture illustrating the events of Acts 2:1-21, including the wind, the tongues of fire, and the people getting excited.

When making such a booklet, draw the first picture on a piece of paper. Next, lay another piece of paper over that one and draw the characters in slightly different positions. Continue in this way until the series of events is completed. Then place the sheets in reverse order (so the first one you drew is on top), staple them together, and flip through them. Youth may want the opportunity to look at one another's booklets. Since this is a unique project, you might want to encourage volunteers to leave their book in a place where people in the congregation can flip through them too!

HINT:
Youth may need to plan the overall action they want to illustrate and how many "frames" they should spend on each. If they want to show (1) wind, (2) fire, and (3) people shouting and raising their hands, and they have 30 pages to use, they might want to allow about ten pages per action.

CONNECT WITH THE BIBLE AND THE FAITH COMMUNITY

A JESUS AND NICODEMUS

Desired Result:
To explore the theme of new life in John 3 or Acts 2.

Bibles, Bible dictionary, concordance, paper, pencils
(Allow 10 minutes.)

Let youth silently read the story of Jesus and Nicodemus in John 3:1-21 with the question in mind, "What ever happened to Nicodemus?" (The Bible does not say, except that he helped to bury Jesus according to John 19:38-42.)

Give each youth a pencil and paper. Ask each person to write a few verses he or she might like to insert in the Bible to satisfy everyone's curiosity about what happened to Nicodemus. For example, did he become a Christian or not? What did he probably say when he ended the conversation with Jesus?

Discuss as a class what may have happened to Nicodemus after this story. If time allows, look up Nicodemus in a Bible dictionary to learn everything you can about him. Also look in a concordance to find out if his name appears anywhere else in the Bible.

B CRAYON PICTURE BANNER

Bibles, crayons, paper
(Allow 10 minutes.)

Give youth paper and crayons. Ask them to read Acts 2:1-21 and create a colorful banner to symbolize the new life that came upon the people and formed the church on Pentecost. Or youth may prefer to create a banner that shows new life or the work of the Holy Spirit in some other way.

Allow the members of your group to symbolize the Holy Spirit in any way they choose. The Holy Spirit is often symbolized by a descending dove or by a flame. Encourage your group members to use what they know about the Holy Spirit and to design their own images or symbols.

When completed, ask volunteers to interpret the symbolism of their banners. Put the banners up around the room.

Desired Result: To explore the theme of new life as it applies to the lives of youth.

CONNECT WITH LIFE

A BY WATER AND BY SPIRIT

paper, markers, hymnals, copies of the Apostles' Creed and the Nicene Creed
(Allow 10 minutes.)

Ask the youth to look in copies of your congregation's hymnal for phrases that talk about our natural birth and also those that talk about our spiritual birth. You may want to suggest that they use the Topical Index to help them with this task. They should also check the hymnal for baptismal services or related responses. Discuss their findings as a group and list them on a large sheet of paper in two columns, one marked "Born of Water" and the other marked "Born of the Spirit."

ASK:

➤ **As you read the baptismal ritual in your congregation's hymnal, does "born of water" mean baptism or being born as a baby? Is it unclear? What do you think Jesus meant when he used this phrase in John 3?** (See especially verse 6 for a good answer.)

ASK:

➤ **Does being baptized mean the same thing as being "born of the spirit"? "born of water"? both? neither? What does it take for a person to be born of the spirit? What changes occur? How can you be "born of the spirit" if you want to be?**

B ZANY ROUNDTABLE DISCUSSION

paper, markers, hymnals, copies of the Apostles' Creed and the Nicene Creed
(Allow 15 minutes.)

Invite four or five adults (not your pastor!) for a roundtable discussion about the Holy Spirit.

Ask one youth be the moderator and the remaining youth to be the audience. Give the moderator a copy of the discussion questions and have him or her ask the panel those questions. Let the audience ask follow-up questions only after all participants have had a chance to respond to each of the zany discussion questions.

Members of the roundtable panel can question one another or disagree with one another. In fact, one of the tasks of the moderator is to "stir up" a little conflict among the participants in the roundtable. The members of the audience should also raise questions and issues that might press the members of the panel, challenge them, or seriously question their understanding of the Holy Spirit. (Of course, you will want to explain all of this to the adults you invite to be the panel. Tell them they will be responding to questions about the Holy Spirit, but do not give them the questions in advance.)

DISCUSSION QUESTIONS

1. If you met the Holy Spirit in person and were given the opportunity to ask any one question, what question would you ask the Holy Spirit and why?

2. If you could choose one animal to become the church's symbol for the Holy Spirit, which one would you choose and why?

3. Some people say that one gift of the Spirit is speaking in tongues. Do you think that means a different earthly language than English or a language that no person on earth could speak or understand without God's help?

4. What is the point, in your opinion, of speaking in tongues? If you had the chance to do it, would you want to?

5. Sometimes the Holy Spirit is symbolized by wind or fire. What difference would it make to the church if the Holy Spirit were symbolized instead by a gentle snowfall? What would that image suggest about the Holy Spirit and would it be true? What does the image of fire and wind make you think of, and what does that tell you about the Holy Spirit?

6. Compare what the Apostles' Creed affirms about the Holy Spirit with all of the things it says about God and Jesus. (Be sure to have copies of the Apostles' Creed available either in your church's hymnal or from the YouthPage in Unit 1 (page 74). Why doesn't the creed say more about the Holy Spirit? Is there anything you would like to add? What?

7. What does the phrase (the Holy Spirit as) "the giver of life" in the Nicene Creed mean to you? (Also make sure that you have copies of the Nicene Creed available from your hymnal or other source.)

8. If we took seriously the fact that the Holy Spirit is really in this room and always present with us no matter where we go, what are the key differences it would make in the way we live our lives?

Desired Result:
To celebrate the new life God gives us.

CLOSING CONNECTIONS

A CREATE A RAP, SONG, OR POEM

paper, markers, Bibles
(Allow 10 minutes.)

Ask youth to create a musical or poetic statement that would answer Nicodemus' question about what it means to be born again. The statement should say something about spiritual new life. Youth may use one of the following as a model for their statement:

- the song "Happy Birthday to You"
- the song "Here Comes the Bride"
- the poem "Roses are Red, Violets are Blue"
- a rap

If youth wish to make up their own poem or song, they can do that, too. Have volunteers read or sing their creation to the class.

ASK:

➤ **How might such a poem, simple song, or rap help other people understand something about the Holy Spirit?**

Ask each group member who developed a song, rap, or poem to "try it out" on someone during this week, asking the hearer what additional questions she or he might have about the Holy Spirit, having heard the rap, poem, or song.

Hint: Can we ever say all there is to be said about the Holy Spirit? Or about God? Or about Christ?

B COME, HOLY SPIRIT!

YouthPage, pencils
(Allow 5 minutes.)

Invite the group members to look at the prayer outline on the YouthPage. Ask each persons to read this outline silently, pausing at each of the blanks and asking God to direct what should go in each blank. Tell group members to be free to add to the prayer outline in any way they wish. (For example, the prayer outline does not include confession for sins.)

Now invite the youth to go back over the prayer outline carefully, filling in each blank as a result of silently praying for God's direction. Ask each group member to silently read her or his prayer when all the blanks are filled, offering it as a gift and a prayer to God.

Conclude the session by asking a volunteer to read his or her prayer aloud to dismiss the class.

Read Me

THIS IS WHAT YOU NEED TO KNOW ABOUT THE TOPIC.

NICODEMUS: THE REST OF THE STORY

During this session, the youth are asked to reconstruct an ideal ending for the story of Nicodemus. From the information given in John 3:1-21, the story about Nicodemus ends rather abruptly. However, after the youth have thought about it on their own, fill them in on the rest of the story (even though it is still mighty sketchy):

Remember that Nicodemus was a leader of the Jews, not the sort of man who would normally run after a wandering preacher to see what he had to say. After all, Nicodemus had his standing in the community to consider; he was a well-respected and important man. Some scholars suggest that Nicodemus came to see Jesus at night so that no one would know he wanted to talk to the carpenter from Galilee. (Do we ever "sneak around" to meet Jesus, afraid of what others will say if they "catch us" praying or reading our Bibles?)

Nicodemus (clearly identified as the same person as in John 3) turns up again in John 7:45-52. In that passage, Nicodemus is one of a group of Jewish leaders who are seeking to have Jesus arrested. However, Nicodemus is clearly the dissenting voice in that group. Does that mean he was an undercover Christian? Probably not. But he was certainly sympathetic and even protective of Jesus, and favored hearing him out. Then there is one more glimpse of this same Nicodemus. When Jesus is buried, Nicodemus provides a small fortune in burial spices for Jesus' body and takes them himself to help Joseph of Arimathea prepare Jesus' body for burial. It would be hard to interpret this gesture in any other way than an act of love and devotion. Yet it still leaves the question up in the air: Did Nicodemus ever really profess faith in Christ and seek to follow him? In the end, it is not necessary for us to know. God knows, and that is enough.

TWO BIRTHS?

In John 3:1-17, Jesus stresses that we all have "two births," and as a result, two lives. The first birth is physical, and ultimately the less important. It is a temporary life. The other "birth" is spiritual. Without Christ, we are dead in our sins. But with him, we live a new and eternal life.

Acts 2:1-42 is about the birth of the church. Churches also have two lives. One is physical. Most church histories that are written, ironically, focus on the progression of buildings: the first one was built on the present site in 1856, followed by a parsonage in 1901, and a new sanctuary in 1939 after the first one proved too small, and so on. But like our physical bodies, the church is much more than just a building. In fact, it is even more than the people. Although the people in Acts had gathered for worship, the church was not really born until the Holy Spirit of God descended upon them. It was then that they "came to life." God's Spirit excited and enlivened them, making them effective preachers and witnesses of the message of Jesus Christ. The church also has a spiritual birth and life is demonstrated by the Spirit of God working through people. That "life" of the church has never died—in fact, it has grown over the centuries to reach around the world, and it is still growing.

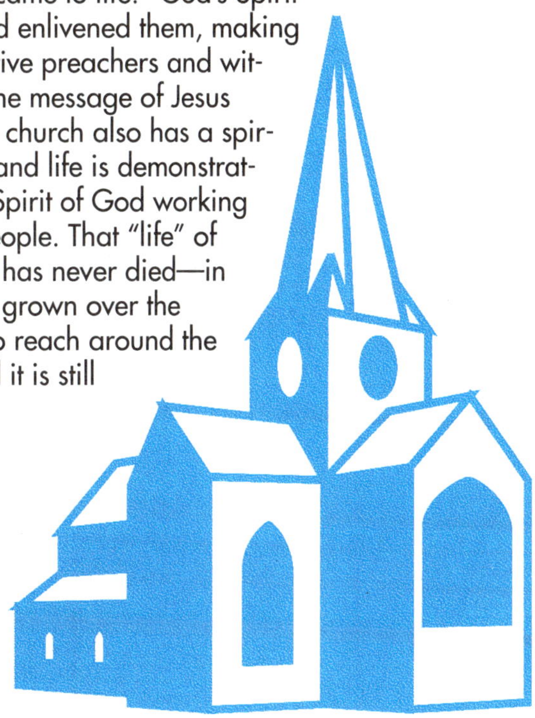

Design Your Own Prayer

To complete the prayer below, circle one of the choices that appear in the parentheses. When there is a blank, fill it in with words of your own. If there is something you don't want to include in your prayer, cross it out. Also feel free to add any sections that you wish.

Dear (Lord, Holy Spirit, Almighty God),

Today I come before you to give you thanks for:

Recently I have been studying about the Holy Spirit, and it has made me appreciate (your love, your guidance, your comforting presence) **more in my life. I would like to thank you for that, too, and for the chance to learn more about you.**

I know that there are many people who may be feeling sad today. Please be with

to comfort them in their time of need. If there is someone feeling lonely or like nobody cares for them, please be with them to help them know of your love. If possible, use me in your comforting work.

I know that in the next few years, I will be facing many decisions that are very important in my life. Some of them that I hope you will help me with are:

I realize that there are many potential pitfalls in life and ways that the wrong decisions can lead to bad consequences. I need your guidance, and pray that you will give me the wisdom I need to make good choices in life.

As I look back at my life, I realize that you have always there for me. Help me find ways to grow closer to you. Some that I would like to try are:

I ask you to give me the courage and determination to do these things. It is great to know that you will always be there for me in the future, and that there is no way I can mess up so badly that you would abandon me. You must love me a lot; help me grow closer to you, so I can feel your (love, acceptance, forgiveness, comfort, peace) **in my daily life.**

Lord, please be with me. All this I pray in Jesus' name. Amen.

THE POTTER AND THE CLAY

SESSION 1: GOD CREATES
SESSION 2: GOD REDEEMS
SESSION 3: GOD VALUES ALL PEOPLE
SESSION 4: TO OBEY AND TO SEE

Purpose:

To explore the biblical image of clay in order to help youth understand and experience God as the one who creates, saves, and values all humankind.

This Is Not Junk Mail!

IT'S IMPORTANT STUFF FROM YOUR TEENAGER'S SUNDAY MORNING LEADER

Raising a junior high youth is a delight AND a challenge. At this stage your young teen is likely to be very energetic. Younger adolescents need lots of physical activity! A teen of this age is also learning how to be a part of groups beyond the family. And you, as a parent, may be experiencing some tension when peer values and family values come into conflict. Your young teen also needs to become more familiar with his or her identity as a separate and unique person. Self-definition is an important developmental task.

Your youth's class is exploring the images of clay in Job 4:17-19; 10:8-9; 33:6; 38:12-14; Isaiah 29:16; 45:8-9; Jeremiah 18:1-6; and Romans 9:20-25. These biblical texts all use the image of clay to present God as the potter and humans as clay. Three of the sessions in the unit focus on God as the one who creates, redeems, and values all creation. The fourth session examines the story from John 9:1-7 where Jesus restores the sight of the man born blind by putting clay or mud on the man's eyes. This last session serves as a summary of many of the themes covered in this unit of CONNECT. This session addresses the way in which our faith informs our actions and our choices, the way in which God is ever present with us through the Holy Spirit and guides us through our daily lives, and finally, the way in which God the Potter works to continually create and redeem us.

Perhaps the most powerful image for middle school youth is the image of God presented in Jeremiah 18:1-6. In this passage Jeremiah reveals God as the one who can take spoiled and damaged clay and reshape it into a new vessel. All humans make mistakes and sin. Often young teens have very intense feelings about the mistakes they make, even when making mistakes is a natural part of growing up or of learning a new skill. The image of God as re-shaper or re-creator can be of great value when a youth feels bad about mistakes.

Spend family time reading and talking about each of the Scriptures. You may have to snag time "in route" from one activity to another in your busy family life, but taking the time will be valuable. Ask questions like:

- **How do you understand God?**
- **What does the image of the potter and the clay say to you about God? about people?**
- **When did you need to be "reshaped" by God?**

Examine the way you think and feel about your young teenager. How do your thoughts and feelings compare with those of God as presented in the Scriptures about clay and potter? Do you feel the need to "reshape" your daughter or son? Do you communicate how much you value your teenager? Do you accept your child's unique personality attributes and communicate how much you appreciate those attributes?

Spend some time praying about these issues. In the space below list actions you can take to communicate how much you care for your young person.

Offer a prayer of gratitude to God for the gift of your young person.

Hallelujah!

IDEAS FOR PEOPLE WHO PLAN WORSHIP

WORSHIP IDEAS

The middle school youth in your church are exploring the biblical images of clay as presented in Job 4:17-19; 10:8-9; 33:6; 38:12-l4; Isaiah 29:16; 45:8-9; Jeremiah 18:1-6; and Romans 9:20-25. These images present portraits of God as the One who creates, redeems, and values all creation. In response to God's graciousness, we are called to a deeper love of God, self, and neighbor.

The Book of Job wrestles with the question of human suffering. Job asks the question that puzzles us all—why does the God who created us allow suffering? The image of clay reveals that human and divine views of human existence are different. Job's friends use the image of clay to express the fragility and sinfulness of human life and God's right and ability to both create and destroy that life. When God speaks in Job 38, the image of clay is used to express God's power to claim and transform human life. This image is more loving than the ones used by Job's friends.

Both Isaiah and Jeremiah emphasize God as the Creator who molds and shapes us, and who, according to Jeremiah, can also reshape and redeem broken, damaged, and spoiled clay. In Romans, Paul uses the image of the potter and clay to affirm the value of both Jews and non-Jews, and in so doing, he helps people more broadly comprehend God as the Creator who values all humans of all cultures.

Try using these biblical texts in worship. You might also write litanies based upon the texts, like the one that follows:

LEADER: Will what is molded say to the one who molds it, "Why have you made me like this?"

PEOPLE: GOD, YOU MADE ME THE WAY I AM BECAUSE YOU LOVE WHO I AM.

LEADER: Has the potter no right over the clay, to make out of the same lump one object for special use and another for ordinary use?

PEOPLE: GOD, YOU GIVE US DIFFERENT TALENTS. ALL HAVE VALUE. "ORDINARY" AND "SPECIAL" ARE HUMAN CATEGORIES.

ALL: TEACH US TO GIVE OUR HEARTS AND MINDS TO YOU. TEACH US TO BELIEVE IN YOUR LOVE FOR US. TEACH US TO LOVE OTHERS.

You might invite a potter to work on a pot as someone reads the Scriptures. The pastor could develop a sermon while the potter works or have the congregation "listen" with clay. Give the worshippers a small lump of modeling clay and ask them to shape their lumps of clay while the Scriptures are read aloud. You might also have the worshippers create symbols of God's love and bring those forward to the altar at some time during worship. Clay can be used to create a powerful symbol of forgiveness and re-creation in God's hands. Worshippers can bring to mind issues that need to be "reshaped" by God, make a clay sculpture that represents those issues, and bring those to the altar. Use hymns such as "Have Thine Own Way, Lord," and "Spirit of the Living God, Fall Afresh On Me" during worship.

Miscellany

IDEAS FOR TEACHERS

WHEN ALL THE YOUTH ARE IN ONE CLASS

Diversity of age and development are key issues when all the youth are in one group. A teacher has the challenge of simultaneously meeting the needs of very different teenagers. Many of the developmental needs of a middle school youth are different from those of an older youth. Analytical skills often differ widely between older and younger teens. Learning styles vary from one youth to another. Some youth will be able to think and converse in an adult fashion while other youth need to move around and expend physical energy.

ALIKE & DIFFERENT

All of the biblical images of clay used in this unit can help youth comprehend God's love for human beings in all of our infinite diversity. We are both alike and different, just as an infinite variety of different objects can all be made from the same lump of clay. The differences among the youth in your class can be a wonderful example of that variety. But also strive to discover the ways in which the youth in your class are alike.

You might want to do additional activities to help your group members identify how they are the same and how they are different. Designate one side of your learning area as "alike" and the other side as "different." Tell the youth that you will read a series of statements aloud. Ask the those group members who believe the statement is true of all youth to stand in the "alike" area. Group members who do not think the statement represents all youth should stand in the "different" area.

SAY:

- Youth love to eat.
- Youth have talents.
- Youth have conflict with parents.
- Youth join cliques.
- Youth need friends.
- Youth love stylish, name-brand clothes.
- Youth want to know about God.
- Youth want to be accepted.
- Youth worry about violence.
- Youth want to help others.
- Youth just want to have fun.
- Youth love music.
- Youth love MTV.

After the game, invite the youth to tell why they chose "alike" or "different" for each statement. Ask the following questions to stimulate discussion about age:

- Do you think youth are more alike or more different at the age of 12? at age17? Explain your answers.
- In what ways do you think youth of different ages are alike?
- In what ways do you think youth of different ages are different?

SESSION 1:
GOD CREATES

FOCUS

To help youth explore the images of clay in the Book of Job.

SCRIPTURE

Job 4:17-19; 10:8-9; 33:6; 38:12-14

HERE'S THE PLAN — DO IT YOUR WAY

OPTIONS	TIME (minutes)	PREPARATION	SUPPLIES
INITIAL CONNECTION			
A Clay Pot Relay Race	10	set up an area to hold the race	modeling clay, tables, masking tape
B "Do I Care?"	8		modeling clay
CONNECT WITH THE SESSION			
A "Listen" With Clay	8	make copies of the YouthPage	clay, YouthPage, Bibles
B Mime the Story of Job	10	make copies of the YouthPage	YouthPage, Bible
C A Clay Tableau	10	make copies of the YouthPage	YouthPage, Bibles, modeling clay
CONNECT WITH THE BIBLE AND THE FAITH COMMUNITY			
A Find Your Scripture	10	prepare index cards with descriptions of how the Bible uses the image of clay (do not include the actual Scripture reference on the card)	index cards, Bibles
B Hear the Book of Job	15		Bibles
CONNECT WITH LIFE			
A What Is the Meaning of *Create*?	8	draw a large outline of a clay pot on the chalkboard or a large sheet of paper.	chalkboard and chalk, or large white paper and markers
B Create a Clay Sculpture	10-12		modeling clay
CLOSING CONNECTION			
Pray for God's Guidance	5	create a small altar by covering the table with the cloth and placing a cross and an interesting piece of pottery on it	a small table, cloth, an interesting piece of clay pottery, a small cross

INITIAL CONNECTION

A CLAY POT RELAY RACE

Have the class form two or more teams. On one side of the room designate a starting line using masking tape. Clear a path to the other side of the room (or to a place at least several feet away) and set up as many tables as there are teams. Put enough modeling clay on the tables for each of the team members.

Each person must run to the table, take a piece of clay, and use it to form a clay pot. That person leaves the pot on the table, then runs back and tags the next team member who will repeat the process. The first team to complete the process—each member making a clay pot in turn—wins.

B PLAY "DO I CARE?"

Have the youth form a circle. Give each youth a lump of modeling clay. Allow the group members time to make a simple sculpture. When everyone has finished, have each person pass his or her sculpture to the person on his or her left. Tell each person to smash the sculpture he or she just received and then return the sculpture to the person who made it.

ASK:

➤ **How did you feel when you smashed someone else's sculpture?**

➤ **How did you feel when someone else smashed your sculpture?**

SAY:

➤ **Imagine that you do not care at all for the sculpture you made. Do something with the sculpture that shows that you do not care. Now imagine that you care deeply for your sculpture. Do something with your sculpture that shows that you care.**

Desired Result:
To experience physical activity and the shaping of clay.
(Choose Activity A or B.)

modeling clay, masking tape, tables
(Allow 10 minutes.)

NOTE TO THE TEACHER!
If feelings run high during this relay, praise both teams and make both winners. For example, "Team A was faster, but Team B made more interesting pots!"

modeling clay
(Allow 8 minutes.)

Desired Result:
To explore the biblical backgrounds that inform the use of clay images in Job.
(Choose Activity A, B, or C.)

CONNECT WITH THE SESSION

A "LISTEN" WITH CLAY

clay, YouthPage, Bibles
(Allow 8 minutes.)

Give each group member a small lump of clay. Have a volunteer read aloud the section entitled "Clay" on the YouthPage. Invite the group to discuss the current uses of clay.

Read aloud the section entitled "God Creates" on the YouthPage. Ask the youth to use the lump of clay you gave them to reenact the Genesis story of the creation of a human beings as they listen to you read.

ASK:

➤ **What does the clay image say to you about the relationship between God and what God creates?**

Read aloud or tell the story of Job using Job 1 and 2 or "Job's Story" on the YouthPage (page 129).

B MIME THE STORY OF JOB

YouthPage, Bible
(Allow 10 minutes.)

NOTE TO THE TEACHER!
Use a modern translation of the Book of Job for this reading. *Today's English Version* or the *Contemporary English Version,* might be easier for your youth to comprehend that the *King James Version* or even the *Revised Standard Version.*

Have a youth read aloud "Clay" on the YouthPage. Have another youth read aloud "God Creates" from the YouthPage. Ask the rest of the group members to listen carefully for new insights or ideas.

ASK:

➤ **What does the concept of clay, especially as it was used in biblical times, say to you about the relationship between God and what God creates?**

➤ **What might be a contemporary image that we could use instead of clay?**

Assign the following roles to the youth: God, Satan, Job, Job's children, Job's wife, and Job's friends. Tell them to act out the parts as you read aloud Job 1–2.

C A CLAY TABLEAU

YouthPage, Bibles, modeling clay
(Allow 10 minutes.)

Have a youth read aloud "Clay" on the YouthPage. Have another youth read aloud "God Creates."

ASK:

- ➤ **What does the concept of clay, especially as it was used in biblical times, say to you about the relationship between God and what God creates?**
- ➤ **What might be a contemporary image that we could use instead of clay?**

Have the youth form three or more teams. Assign one of the following scenes from Job 1 and 2 to each team: 1) the heavenly council; 2) Job receives news of his children's death; 3) Job and his wife; 4) Job and his friends. Tell the teams to use the modeling clay to recreate the scenes. Have each team tell about its sculpture and what it represents.

CONNECT WITH THE BIBLE AND THE FAITH COMMUNITY

Desired Result:
To explore the specific uses of clay imagery in Job and what this image suggests about the nature of God.

(Choose Option A or B.)

A FIND YOUR SCRIPTURE

index cards, Bibles
(Allow 10 minutes.)

S

Give the following Scriptures to three of the group members, one Scripture to a youth: Job 4:17-19; 10:8-9; 33:6; and 38:12-14. Have the remaining teens form four teams. (A team can be one person, if your group is small.) Write on index cards the descriptions listed below of the way the Scriptures use the image of clay. (The Scripture reference is in parentheses for your information. Do not include the Scripture reference on the card.)

> Humans are clay houses. (Job 4:17-19)
> God formed humans as from clay. (Job 10:8-9)
> Elihu, like Job, was formed of clay. (Job 33:6)
> Sunrise changes the earth like a seal changes clay. (Job 38:12-14)

Tell the three youth who were assigned passages to find their Scripture passage and to read it aloud over and over. Each of the four teams has an index card with a summary of one of the four Scriptures passages on it. The task of each team is to identify the person reading the Scripture that is summarized on its card. (Remember: Four people will be reading and rereading their Scripture aloud simultaneously; the teams will have to listen carefully.) After all the teams have found the person reading their Scripture aloud, have the teams discuss the following questions about their particular Scripture passage:

- ➤ **Who is the speaker in this Scripture?**
- ➤ **What does the clay image say about humans? about God?**
- ➤ **What attitude do you think the speaker has about humans? about God?**

Bibles
(Allow 15 minutes.)

S

B HEAR THE BOOK OF JOB

Give the following Scriptures to four youth, one Scripture to a youth: Job 4:17-19; 10:8-9; 33:6. Have the youth assigned Job 4:17-19 read these verses aloud.

ASK:
- **Who is the speaker in this Scripture?**
- **What does the clay image say about humans? about God?**
- **What attitude do you think the speaker has about humans? about God?**

SAY:
- **As a group,work quickly to put this passage into your own words. Think about what modern images and ideas you would include that still emphasize what this passage says about humans and about God.**

Repeat the process for the other two Scriptures. Then tell the group members to close their eyes and listen as you read Job 38:12-14. Ask them to try to visualize the images as you read.

ASK:
- **Who is the speaker?**
- **What does the clay image say about humans? about God?**
- **What attitude do you think the speaker has about humans? about God?**
- **How is this Scripture different from the other three?**

CONNECT WITH LIFE

Desired Result:
To explore how the understanding of a Creator who loves the creation can help youth discover and develop their God-given gift to create.
(Choose Activity A, or B.)

A WHAT IS THE MEANING OF *CREATE?*

chalkboard and chalk or a large sheet of paper and markers
(Allow 8 minutes.)

Ahead of time, draw a large outline of a clay pot on the chalkboard or on a large sheet of paper.

SAY:
- **To create means to cause something to exist. Think of something you have made. It might be a painting, drawing, sculpture or other work of art. It might be a piece of music you have memorized or composed. It might be a meal you have cooked. It might be something you have written. Or it might be an attractive space you created when you put things in order in your room. Describe it.**

Invite the youth to tell about the things they have created. Affirm each creation. List the identified creation inside the outline of the clay pot you drew earlier.

ASK:

➤ **How did you feel or what did you think about what you created? How did you feel as you were making this creation? How did you feel when it was completed? What did completing it make you want to do next?**

➤ **Have you ever made a new friend?**

➤ **How can a new friendship be an act of creation?**

➤ **How do you "create" a friendship?**

➤ **How can helping others be an act of creation?**

➤ **What other actions might be viewed as actions that create?**

B CREATE A CLAY SCULPTURE

modeling clay
(Allow 10-12 minutes.)

Divide your group into pairs. Give each pair a lump of modeling clay. Tell each pair to create a sculpture that shows how the two people in the pair might use their talents and aptitudes to "create" a better world. This will require conversation, compromise, and cooperation within the pairs. When the teams have finished their creation, invite them to tell about their sculptures.

CLOSING CONNECTION

PRAY FOR GOD'S GUIDANCE

Desired Result:
To worship together.

a small table, cloth, an interesting piece of clay pottery, a small cross
(Allow 5 minutes.)

Ahead of time, create a small altar by covering a table with a cloth and placing a cross and an interesting piece of pottery on it.

SAY:

➤ **God created you. God gave you gifts. God loves you. You are created to create. God calls you to help create a more loving world.**

Invite the youth to gather near the altar and to spend a few moments praying silently about what God would like them to do in order to create a more loving world. If you did activity B above, invite them to place their clay sculptures on the altar as a symbol of their willingness to help create a more loving world. Close the session with the following prayer:

> **God, you made us. You love us. You need us. We want to help create a more loving world. Thank you for showing us how. In Christ we pray, Amen.**

Read Me THIS IS WHAT YOU NEED TO KNOW ABOUT THE TOPIC.

Creator & Creation

This unit explores the image of the potter and the clay as an image of God as the One who creates, loves, and reshapes the creation. As a part of creation, humans are loved and continually reshaped by God. God's creative activity is bountiful, kaleidoscopic, and full of wonder. It never ceases, but goes on all around us, everywhere, everyday.

We can choose to participate in God's wondrous creative activity. Our acts become part of God's creative acts when they contribute to a greater love of God, self, and neighbor. As we contribute to beauty, truth, mercy, and justice, we create. Just as we were created in the image of God, we are called to create and to love creation just as God creates and loves creation.

Being "creative" is much more than simply being able to draw, sing, sew, or build things. New friendships, new communities, new ideas, new sounds, new spaces are all acts of creation. A person can be creative in any human activity.

Read the Scriptures for this session. Read the "Bible Background" below. Take a few minutes to consider the following questions and record your responses:

- **How are you creative?**
- **How can you help create a more loving world?**

Think about the youth in your class. How are they creative? How can the image of potter and clay help them discover their value in God's eyes? Pray for them. Ask for God's guidance as you prepare the session for them.

Bible Background

The image of God as potter and humans as clay occurs numerous times in the book of Job. The book of Job begins with an ancient story about God permitting Satan to bring harm to Job in order to test Job's faithfulness to God. Job loses his children, his fortune, and his health. The writer of Job challenges the idea that people who are faithful and obedient to God will not suffer, and the notion that suffering is punishment for disobedience. Job's friends join him on the ash heap to comfort him in his despair and to convince Job of his need to repent. Within this context, Eliphaz, Job, and Elihu present God the Creator by using the image of a potter who fashions clay (Job 4, 10, and 33, respectively). These passages echo the creation story in Genesis 1 and 2. We, who are formed from the dust of the earth, are created in the image of God and are a part of God's good creation.

Eliphaz, one of Job's friends, asks him: *"Is not your fear of God your confidence, and the integrity of your ways your hope? Think now, who that was innocent ever perished? Or where were the upright cut off?" (Job 4:6-7).*

Eliphaz speaks about human existence as a clay house in order to differentiate between humans and the Creator (4:17-19). Humans are mortal; God is immortal. Only God is righteous. Job expresses his faith that the Creator loves the creation and would not allow it to suffer as he cries out to God: *"Your hands fashioned and made me; and now you turn and destroy me. Remember that you fashioned me like clay; and will you turn me to dust again?" (Job 10:8-9).*

Elihu uses the clay image (33:6) to establish his equality with Job: both are created by God from the dust of the earth.

God, on the other hand, uses the image of clay to express transformation:

> *Have you commanded the morning since your days began, and caused the dawn to know its place, so that it might take hold of the skirts of the earth, and the wicked be shaken out of it? It is changed like clay under the seal, and it is dyed like a garment.*
>
> *(Job 38:12 14).*

This breathtaking image is not destructive; it is transformational. The dawn changes the earth in the way the seal changes the shape of clay or dye changes the color of a garment. From the human perspective, a clay structure is temporary and subject to destruction. From the divine perspective, the shape and form we have is a gift from God our Creator.

CLAY

Clay is a form of dirt that is mixed with water to make pottery, bricks, sculptures, toys, and writing tablets. In ancient times a special ring was pressed into a lump of clay to show ownership. The image of the potter and the clay is used several times in the Book of Job to represent God as the One who creates and reshapes humans.

God Creates

> *God saw everything that he had made, and indeed, it was very good.*
> *(Genesis 1 :31)*

> *The LORD God formed man from the dust of the ground, and breathed into his nostrils the breath of life; and the man became a living being.*
> *(Genesis 2:7)*

The understanding of God as Creator gives texture to the story of Job. God creates. Creation is good. God loves the creation.

Job's Story

The book of Job begins with an ancient story of a man who worships God and turns away from evil. At a meeting of the heavenly council, God identifies Job as one who is righteous.

Satan challenges God, arguing that Job's righteousness depends upon Job's good fortune. If Job suffered, Satan continues, surely Job would curse God. God permits Satan to take away all Job's wealth and to kill Job's sons and daughters. Job does not blame God. Next, Satan is allowed to cover Job's body with boils. As Job sits in the ashes and scrapes his boils, his wife suggests that he curse God and die. Job refuses and remains faithful to God. Three friends, Bildad, Zophar, and Eliphaz wish to console Job. They sit silently in the ashes with Job for seven days.

As Job and his friends discuss Job's plight, they speak about human beings as clay that is easily broken or destroyed. God speaks about clay as being reshaped into an identifying clay seal. The divine view of humans is more hopeful and more loving than our own view of ourselves!

SESSION 2:

GOD REDEEMS

FOCUS

To help youth explore how Isaiah and Jeremiah use the image of the potter and the clay to portray God as the One who redeems and restores all of creation.

SCRIPTURE

Isaiah 29:16; 45:8-9
Jeremiah 18:1-6

HERE'S THE PLAN DO IT YOUR WAY

OPTIONS	TIME (minutes)	PREPARATION	SUPPLIES
INITIAL CONNECTION			
Reshape the Clay	8-10	prepare the instructions for the activity on pieces of paper; arrange pieces of paper on the floor in the shape of a path; buy treats or small gift items to give the winning team	modeling clay, twenty or thirty sheets of paper, one die from a pair of dice, small treats
CONNECT WITH THE SESSION			
A Reshape a Sculpture	5		YouthPage, modeling clay
B "Broken Pot" Puzzle	5	make a large clay pot or pitcher out of modeling clay and disassemble it by cutting it into pieces before it dries	modeling clay
CONNECT WITH THE BIBLE AND FAITH COMMUNITY			
A "Talking Pot" Skits	15		Bibles, Read Me
B Giant Comic Strips	15	make copies of "Bible Background" on Read Me	two long sheets of paper or newsprint, markers, Bibles, YouthPage, Read Me
CONNECT WITH LIFE			
A News Stories	10	collect a variety of stories from newspapers	clippings of newspaper stories
B Life Situations	8	write life situation examples on slips of paper	slips of paper, bowl or basket
CLOSING CONNECTION			
Pray Together	5	make copies of the YouthPage	paper and pencils, YouthPage

INITIAL CONNECTION

RESHAPE THE CLAY

Write the following instructions on sheets of paper, one instruction to a sheet:

- **You have dropped and smashed your clay pot! Reshape it.**
- **You became so frustrated with a homework assignment that you smashed your fist on your desk, hitting your clay pot by accident and mashing it flat! Reshape it.**
- **A cat stepped on your clay pot before it was dry! Reshape it.**
- **Your little brother mistook your clay pot for a basketball. After having been thrown against the backboard several times, your pot needs to be reshaped!**
- **A jogger ran over your clay pot flat! Reshape it.**
- **You left your pot on a railroad track by mistake. Of course, a train ran over it! Reshape it.**
- **A football team mistook your clay pot for a fumbled football. Oops! Reshape the pot.**
- **A drummer thought your clay pot was a snare drum! You'll have to reshape it.**
- **Your mom just came in and said "You left your clay pot in the driveway again! " Looks like it needs to be reshaped.**

Give each group member a small lump of clay and ask each to quickly make a clay pot.

Create a life-sized board game on the floor by arranging twenty to thirty sheets of paper, including those with instructions, in the shape of a path on the floor. Place the sheets with the instructions at random intervals along the path. Place a sheet labeled "home" at the end of the path. Players will move by throwing the die and advancing the number of spaces along the path.

Start with the teen whose last name begins with the letter nearest the end of the alphabet. Have this person throw the die and move forward on the path the number of spaces indicated. If he or she lands on a space with written instructions, he or she must go back to the beginning and reshape his or her clay pot. Group members will take turns in reverse alphabetical order throwing the die and moving along the path. The first youth to get "home" wins a treat for all the group members. This treat can be a small piece of wrapped candy, a bookmark, or some other small recognition. In this way, the entire group benefits from the success of one of its members.

Desired Result:
To provide physical activity and to introduce the theme of redemption.

modeling clay, twenty or thirty sheets of paper, one die from a pair of dice, small treat or gift for winners

(Allow 8-10 minutes.)

Desired Result:
To introduce the concept of reshaping.

(Choose Option A or B.)

YouthPage, modeling clay
(Allow 5 minutes)

CONNECT WITH THE SESSION

A RESHAPE A SCULPTURE

Give each group member a small lump of clay and ask each to make something out of the piece of clay. As they are working on their creation,

ASK:

- **What are you making?**
- **How do you want it to look?**
- **Is it shaping up exactly the way you want it to?**
- **How are you changing it or reshaping it as you make it?**
- **Have you felt the need to start over? Explain.**

Have a youth read aloud "Reshaping Clay" on the YouthPage.

ASK:

- **What do each of these words suggest to you?**

- **What other words suggesting "reshaping" a creation would you add?**

Give the youth a few minutes to finish the activity on the YouthPage. Discuss as a group the words that each person added.

modeling clay
(Allow 5 minutes)

B ASSEMBLE A "BROKEN POT" PUZZLE

Ahead of time, make a large clay pot or pitcher out of modeling clay. Carefully disassemble it by cutting it into several pieces before it is dry. Try to cut the pieces so that they can be easily reassembled into the pot. (If you have trouble with this, try constructing something flat, then cut it apart like a jigsaw puzzle before it is dry.) In effect, you are creating a puzzle from the clay. If you have a large group, make several "broken pot" puzzles.

Mix up the puzzle pieces and distribute them among the youth. Tell them to reassemble the "broken" pot. When the puzzle or puzzles have been reassembled, **ASK:**

- **Have you ever broken something, then fixed it?**
- **What did you break? Do you remember how you felt when you broke it?**
- **How did you fix it?**
- **How did you feel when it was fixed?**

Have a youth read aloud "Reshaping Clay" on the YouthPage.

ASK:

➤ **What do each of these words suggest to you?**

Have the teens think of other words that suggest "reshaping" the creation and write them in the space provided on the YouthPage.

CONNECT WITH THE BIBLE AND THE FAITH COMMUNITY

Desired Result:
To introduce the biblical image of God as the One who has the power to reshape, restore, and transform our lives.

(Choose Option A, B, or C.)

A CREATE "TALKING POT" SKITS

Bibles, Read Me, YouthPage
(Allow 15 minutes.)

S

Have a group member read aloud "Isaiah and Jeremiah Talk About Clay" on the YouthPage. Then ask another group member to read aloud Isaiah 29:16 and another to read aloud Isaiah 45:8-9. In your own words, relate the information about these passages from "Bible Background" and other reading you have undertaken in preparation for this session.

Have the group form teams of three or more. Ask each team to create a skit. One team member will play the role of a potter or sculptor. Each of the other team members will play the role of the "object" that is being created by the potter or sculptor. In the skit the object being created should tell the potter how to create it and how to make it better! Allow about five minutes for the youth to create the skits. Have each team present its skit.

After the teams have presented their skits, **ASK:**

➤ **How did the "sculptors" or "creators" feel about being coached by their creations?**

➤ **How did the "things" being created feel when the sculptor listened to their advice? when the sculptor didn't listen?**

➤ **Have you ever tried to tell someone how she or he ought to do something? What did you tell them?**

➤ **Did you know more about it than that person did? Were you helpful or bossy? How was your advice received?**

➤ **Did you ever think you knew how to do something, then discovered that you didn't know as much as you thought you did? Explain.**

➤ **Have you ever thought or felt that you needed to tell God how to do something? Why or why not?**

➤ **If you could tell God to "fix" something, what would it be?**

Ask a group member to read aloud Jeremiah 18:1-6. In your own words, give the information about this Scripture from "Bible Background" on the Read Me page (page 136-137). Tell each team to "reshape" their skits to illustrate Jeremiah 18:1-6. Encourage the teams to use the skits they have already created rather than simply acting out Jeremiah 18:1-6. The skit should show the creator in charge of the creation rather than the creation in charge of the creator!

ASK:

- **What does it mean to you that God, the potter, can reshape spoiled clay?**
- **What does the image tell you about the way God works in our world, in our community, in our families, and in our personal lives?**

two long sheets of paper, markers, Bibles, YouthPage, Read Me
(Allow 15 minutes.)

B GIANT COMIC STRIPS

Have the group form two teams. Give each team Bibles, markers, and a large sheet of paper. Assign Isaiah 29:16 and 45:8-9 to one team and Jeremiah 18:1-6 to the other team. Make photocopies of "Bible Background" from the Read Me pages (page 136-137) and give a copy to each team. Tell them to read their Scriptures, "Isaiah and Jeremiah Talk About Clay" on the YouthPage, and the section of the "Bible Background" that addresses their particular passage.

DISCUSS:

- **Who is in charge of shaping the clay?**
- **What does your passage suggest is the end result of shaping the clay?**

Have the teams create giant comic strips with three or four frames that are based on these Scriptures. Tell them to be as creative as they can. The comic strips can be drawn with contemporary people if a team desires. Have each team tell about its comic strip and the discussions the team had as the comic strip was being created.

ASK:

- **What does the image of the potter and the clay in Isaiah and Jeremiah tell you about God?**

CONNECT WITH LIFE

Desired Result:
To get youth to consider how God works to restore and redeem us, in spite of our the sinful choices we make.
(Choose Activity A or B.)

clippings of various newspaper stories
(Allow 10 minutes.)

A NEWS STORIES

Ahead of time, collect a variety of stories from newspapers. Divide the group into pairs of teens. Give a different newspaper story to each pair. Invite the pairs to discuss answers to the following questions about their newspaper stories:

- **In what way does the story compare to the image of "spoiled" clay?**
- **How might the "spoiled clay" in this story be reshaped?**
- **What could a person do to reshape the events and consequences of the newspaper story?**

- **How do you see God as the Potter who has the power to reshape the clay in this particular story?**
- **If God can reshape the lives in this story as a potter reshapes the clay, what might happen next in this story?**

Have each pair tell about the assigned newspaper story and how they answered the questions.

B LIFE SITUATIONS

slips of paper, bowl or basket
(Allow 8 minutes.)

S

Before the session, write the following life situations on small pieces of paper, one situation to each piece:

- **Margaret told a lie about her friend Julie.**
- **Jason cheated on an English test and got caught.**
- **A group of boys on the soccer team did not invite one of the players to a party because they didn't like him. He found out and quit the team.**
- **Susan drove her parents' car without permission or a license. She had a wreck and her best friend, who was also in the car, was injured.**
- **Raymond stole a CD from a music store.**
- **Karen took some beer from her parents' refrigerator and invited several of her friends to drink it with her.**

Fold these slips of paper and place them in a bowl or basket. Pass the basket. Have each group member draw a piece of paper out of the basket and read it aloud.

ASK:

- **What are the possible consequences of this situation?**
- **How can God reshape this situation as a potter reshapes clay?**

CLOSING CONNECTION

Desired Result: To offer thanks for God's redemptive power in our lives.

PRAY TOGETHER

paper and pencil, YouthPage
(Allow 5 minutes.)

S

Read aloud the opening paragraph of "The Loving Hands of the Potter" on the YouthPage. Have the youth close their eyes and become aware of God's loving presence. Invite them to imagine God as a loving potter shaping a beautiful piece of clay. Ask the questions in "The Loving Hands of the Potter." Invite the youth to open their eyes and write responses to the questions.

Close the session with the following prayer:

Loving God, you created us and care for us. You have the power to reshape us. We offer ourselves to you now. Thank you for making us into new people. In Christ 's name we pray, Amen.

Read Me

THIS IS WHAT YOU NEED TO KNOW ABOUT THE TOPIC.

Prepare Yourself

Find a comfortable spot away from distractions. Have your Bible, paper, and a pencil handy to make notes. Pray for God's guidance and presence as you prepare for your group. Read Isaiah 29:16 and 45:8-9.

Reflect on occasions in your life when you may have tried to tell God, the Potter, how your life should be shaped. Write any insights here:

Read Jeremiah 18:1-6. When has God reshaped your life?

Read the "Bible Background" below. Do the activities on the YouthPage for yourself. As you prepare, think about the individuals in your group. Do any of them have life issues that may be helped by the knowledge that a loving God reshapes life as a potter reshapes clay?

Pray the following prayer:

> **Loving God, thank your for your power to reshape our lives. Help us all to give ourselves to your love and hope. Guide me as I lead your youth in this session. Help them to know how much you love them. In Christ I pray, Amen.**

BIBLE BACKGROUND

The messages from the books of Isaiah and Jeremiah are best understood against the backdrop of history. The destruction of the Northern Kingdom of Israel with the fall of Samaria to the Assyrians in 722 B.C., and the Babylonian Exile that began with the fall of Jerusalem in the Southern Kingdom of Judah in 587 B.C. raised questions in the people's hearts about God's faithfulness to them.

At the time of the prophets, people believed that blessings were God's rewards for righteousness and that troubles and tribulations were God's direct punishment for sinfulness and unrighteousness. But then as now, people were reluctant to recognize that their own selfishness and self-centeredness had brought about their trials. Politically, the people's inability to work in harmony and genuine cooperation had led to a weakening of the two kingdoms and made them easy targets for any of the surrounding nations bent on conquest. The people of Israel and Judah failed to realize, even though prophets like Isaiah and Jeremiah continually tried to warn them, that they could live in harmony, strength, and peace only as they lived according to God's will.

The time of intense political unrest before the fall of Samaria provides the background for Isaiah 29:16, although Isaiah lived and preached in the Southern Kingdom of Judah whose center was in Jerusalem. The restoration of the people of Judah, those who had been forcibly driven from Jerusalem after the fall of the city and driven into exile in Babylonia, provides the background for Isaiah 45:8-9. This restoration, which the people of Judah saw as God's divine will, was occasioned by the Edict of Cyrus, a law pronounced by the king of Persia that not only permitted but instructed the people of Judah to return to Jerusalem and to rebuild the Temple (2 Chronicles 36:22-23; Ezra 1:1-4).

Both the Isaiah passage and the Jeremiah passage use the image of a potter and clay to remind the people of God's sovereign power. Isaiah points to the arrogance of a people who would place themselves above the one who creates them, and in Isaiah 45:9, reminds the people that it is inappropriate for the "creation" to blame God for the ill that occurs. Using the image of a piece of clay questioning the potter, Isaiah drives home how inappropriate it is to doubt the goodness of God's work. This verse and the accusation it contains follow Isaiah 45:8, an expression of the desire for righteousness and salvation to grow from the earth that God created.

JEREMIAH 18:1-6

The ministry of the prophet Jeremiah began in about 627 B.C. and continued through the fall of Jerusalem to Babylon (587 B.C.) and into the time of Exile. Jeremiah was often in trouble for criticizing Judah and Jerusalem. He spoke about both God's judgment and God's salvation. In Jeremiah 18:6, Jeremiah uses the image of the potter and the clay to help the people understand God's power to create and to save.

Both Isaiah and Jeremiah were sensitive to the political atmosphere of the Northern and Southern Kingdoms. They viewed the suffering of the exiled people as a consequence of disobeying God's law, a law that is intended for the good of the people. The people of both Israel and Judah discover hope only through confession and repentance. The words of the prophets called the people to repent of their sins against God and assured them that even though they have sinned and violated God's will, their lives are not over. They can be remade, recreated, and reshaped by God's love. Like a potter, God creates and God values the creation. The creation, like clay, can be reshaped. God is a God of second chances (and more!).

The Hebrew and Greek words used in the Bible and translated "redeem" mean to release, preserve, deliver, rescue, pay a debt, or buy back a relative's property.

Christians use this word and other words to describe God's action in the world. Other words we use to describe God's actions are recreate, transform, reshape, save, heal, provide new birth. The image of the potter reshaping spoiled clay metaphorically and poetically describes God's redemptive activity in the world and in our lives.

You turn things upside down! Shall the potter be regarded as the clay? Shall the thing made say of its maker, "He did not make me"; or the thing formed say of the one who formed it, "He has no understanding"?

Isaiah 29:16

RESHAPING CLAY

The image of reshaping clay is one way to visualize God's power to change a person's life. Some words Christians use to express this power of God are:

- **redeem**
- **reshape**
- **recreate**
- **transform**
- **save**
- **heal**
- **change**
- **new life**
- **rebirth**

Can you think of other words? Write them below.

Isaiah and Jeremiah Talk About Clay

Both Isaiah and Jeremiah were prophets who called the people to worship God and to practice love, justice, and mercy toward all people. Breaking God's law wounded the whole community by disrupting the harmony and peace God intended for the people. These prophets believed that being conquered (or even the threat of being conquered) by other nations was the consequence of disobeying God's law. Jeremiah and Isaiah believed that repentance or "turning again" to God would restore the community and drive out the enemies of God's people. Like a potter lovingly reshaping spoiled clay, God will graciously redeem and restore the people of Israel and Judah as a nation. God restores and transforms not only individual lives but also nations, kingdoms, and communities.

THE LOVING HANDS OF THE POTTER

Think about something you have done that was not good for you or for another. If you could backtrack, you would do things differently!

- **How did you feel when you realized it was a bad choice? How do you feel now?**
- **How does the action compare to "spoiled clay"?**
- **How can (or did) God reshape this "spoiled clay" in your life?**

HAVE THINE OWN WAY, LORD

One of the much-loved hymns of the Christian church is "Have Thine Own Way, Lord." You may have sung this hymn in church, at camp, or even in your youth group. Read these words as a poem. Notice how the first verse picks up the ideas this session has considered: God is the potter, we are the clay. Try your hand at writing another verse for this poem, but try using a different symbol or image for the potter and the clay.

Have thine own way, Lord! Have thine own way!

Thou art the potter; I am the clay.
Mold me and make me after thy will,
while I am waiting, yielded and still.

Have thine own way, Lord! Have thine own way!

Search me and try me, Savior today!
Wash me just now, Lord, wash me just now,
as in thy presence humbly I bow.

Have thine own way, Lord! Have thine own way!

Wounded and weary, help me I pray!
Power, all power, surely is thine!
Touch me and heal me, Savior divine.

Have thine own way, Lord! Have thine own way!

Hold o'er my being absolute sway.
Fill with thy Spirit till all shall see
Christ only, always, living in me!

Words: Adelaide A. Pollard
Music: George C. Stebbins

SESSION 3:

GOD VALUES ALL PEOPLE

FOCUS

To help youth explore how the apostle Paul uses the image of a potter and clay to demonstrate God's care for all people.

SCRIPTURE

Romans 9:20-25

HERE'S THE PLAN DO IT YOUR WAY

OPTIONS	TIME (minutes)	PREPARATION	SUPPLIES
INITIAL CONNECTION			
"Tell the Sculptor!"	8	make some simple, flat sculptures out of modeling clay	Bible, modeling clay sculptures, paper plates, modeling clay
CONNECT WITH THE SESSION			
A Create Clay Objects	8-10	make copies of YouthPage	YouthPage, modeling clay
B Special and Ordinary	5-8	obtain a matching, ornate serving dish and bowl	an ornate serving dish and bowl, Bibles
CONNECT WITH THE BIBLE AND FAITH COMMUNITY			
A Rainbow Stories	10	cut a large rainbow shape from posterboard, leaving the rainbow uncolored, and tape to a wall or other surface	Bibles, paper, pencil, posterboard, colored markers
B Modeling Clay Mosaic	10		Bibles, several different colors of modeling clay
C Create a Skit	12-15	obtain several colors of clay	Bible, paper, pencil, posterboard, colored markers
CONNECT WITH LIFE			
A Giant Rainbow Collage	8	gather supplies	large sheet of paper or posterboard, old magazines, glue, markers, scissors
B Discuss a TV Show	10		Bibles, paper and pencils
CLOSING CONNECTION			
Pray a Hymn	5		hymnals

INITIAL CONNECTION

PLAY "TELL THE SCULPTOR!"

Desired Result:
To experience physical activity, artistic expression, and positive social interaction.

Bible, modeling clay sculptures, paper plates, modeling clay
(Allow 8 minutes.)

Ahead of time, make some simple, flat sculptures out of modeling clay. Put each sculpture on a separate paper plate. You might make a simple daisy on a stem, a tree, a house, a car, etc. Make one sculpture for every two teenagers in your group.

Have the group break up into pairs. Tell the teens in each pair to sit on the floor back to back. Give one person in each pair one of the paper plates with a sculpture on it, and other person a lump of clay and a paper plate. Make sure this person does not look at the sculpture given to his or her partner. The teen holding the sculpture you made must describe it, without naming the object, to his or her partner so that he or she can recreate it. (How do you describe a tree without saying, "It looks like a tree?") The partner who is sculpting cannot ask questions for clarification. When the sculptor has finished, have the pair compare its sculpture with the original. You should have some interesting contrasts!

Read aloud Romans 9:20.

CONNECT WITH THE SESSION

Desired Result:
To explore Paul's image of clay in Romans 9:21. **(Choose Activity A or B.)**

A CREATE CLAY OBJECTS

YouthPage, modeling clay, Bibles
(Allow 8-10 minutes.)

Have a youth read aloud Romans 9:21.

Give each youth a lump of clay. Tell them to divide the lump into two pieces. Have each group member create something ornate and special with one half and something simple and functional with the other half. When everyone is finished, have the youth tell about their objects.

Tell the members of the class to write responses to the questions in "The Same Lump of Clay" on the YouthPage. Use their responses to stimulate discussion. Then have a group member read aloud "Does God Love My Talents or Me?"

B SPECIAL AND ORDINARY

a serving dish and a bowl from the same set of china
(Allow 5-8 minutes.)

Have a youth read Romans 9:21 aloud. Tell about the serving dish and the bowl as two objects created from the "same lump of clay," one for special use and the other for ordinary everyday use.

Desired Result:
To explore Paul's understanding of God's love for all people in Romans 9:22-25.
(Choose Option A, B, or C.)

Bibles, paper, pencil, posterboard, colored markers
(Allow 10 minutes.)

Teacher Note!

Some of your group members may know the scientific reason why a rainbow is so many colors—the refraction of sunlight through water vapor, etc. But this is not what this activity is seeking. Allow group members to use their imaginations to come up with the most creative stories and reasons as to why the rainbow is multi-colored.

ASK:

➤ **Do you think one of these dishes is more important than the other? Explain.**
➤ **What do you think "special" means? Give some examples.**
➤ **What do you think "ordinary" means? Give some examples.**
➤ **Tell about a time when you felt special.**
➤ **Tell about a time when you felt ordinary.**
➤ **Were you of more value when you were "special" than when you were "ordinary"? In whose eyes? yours? your friends'? your parents'? God's?**

Have the youth write responses to the questions in "The Same Lump of Clay" on the YouthPage. Discuss their responses.

Have a youth read aloud "Does God Love My Talents or Me?"

CONNECT WITH THE BIBLE AND THE FAITH COMMUNITY

A RAINBOW STORIES

Ahead of time, cut a large rainbow shape from the posterboard. Leave the rainbow uncolored. Tape it on a wall or other surface for all to see. Have the class members form teams of three or four. Tell each team that its assignment will be to make up a story about the creation of the rainbow.

Ask the teens imagine that God has given the angels the assignment of deciding how God should create a rainbow. These angels are having difficulty deciding what color to make the rainbow. Each team's story should answer the question, "Why is the rainbow so many different colors?" When the teams have finished, have them read or tell their stories aloud.
Read aloud Romans 9:22-25.

ASK:

➤ **What does Paul mean by the "riches of God's glory"?**
➤ **How do you experience them?**

Using the colored markers, write brief responses on the rainbow poster.

SAY:

➤ **Paul understood that God creates and accepts all people. God's glory shows through all people.**

ASK:

➤ **How do you see God's glory in people?**
➤ **Do you have trouble seeing God's glory in some kinds of people? What kinds? Why?**
➤ **How can you begin to see God's glory even in these people?**
➤ **Where and how do you see God's glory in yourself?**

B MODELING CLAY MOSAIC

Bibles, several different colors of modeling clay ***(Allow 10 minutes.)***

Have a youth read aloud Romans 9:22-25.

ASK:
- **What does Paul mean by the "riches of God's glory"?**
- **How do you experience them?**

SAY:
- **Paul understood that God creates and accepts all people. God's glory shows through all people.**

ASK:
- **How do you see God's glory in people? in yourself?**

Have the youth form teams of three or four. Give each team several colors of modeling clay. Have the teams create a clay mosaic that represents the way God's glory can shine through all people. A mosaic uses small pieces of objects of different colors to create a large, harmonious picture.

C CREATE A SKIT

Bibles, paper, pencils, poster paper, colored markers ***(Allow 12-15 minutes.)***

Do activity A, "Write Rainbow Stories," as described above. Then have the youth create and perform skits based on their stories.

CONNECT WITH LIFE

S

Desired Result:
To make connections between contemporary life and the expression of God's love for all people in Romans 9:25.
(Choose Activity A or B.)

A GIANT RAINBOW COLLAGE

large sheet of paper or posterboard, old magazines, glue, markers, scissors ***(Allow 8 minutes.)***

Do Activity 3A, "Write a Rainbow Story" as described above.

ASK:
- **What do you think the world would be like today if all people were the same?**
- **What do you think the world would be like today if God loved only one group of people?**

Give each youth an old magazine. Have each teen look through the magazine and cut out pictures of people. Have the class glue all the pictures collected on a large sheet of paper or posterboard to create a rainbow-shaped collage.

Read aloud Romans 9:25: "Those who were not my people I will call 'my people,' and her who was not beloved I will call 'beloved.'" Have the youth write this verse on the collage.

Bibles, paper and pencils
(Allow 10 minutes.)

S

B DISCUSS A TV SHOW

Read aloud Romans 9:25. Have the group form two or more teams. Tell the teams to imagine that they are writers for a TV show set in a high school. Ask each team to discuss and write an outline of a TV show about a teenager who at first feels unloved and unaccepted, but something happens to change these feelings. Each team must decide what action brings about this change, why it occurs, and how it happens.

Ask the teams to use these questions to help them plan their shows.

- **Who is the teen who feels unaccepted?**
- **Why does the teen feel unloved and unwanted?**
- **Who are the classmates of the teenager?**
- **Do the classmates like or dislike the teen who feels so unloved? Why?**
- **What happens in the story to change the way the teen feels?**
- **How does the TV show you are outlining illustrate Romans 9:25?**
- **What do you think your show says about God's love for the "unaccepted"?**

Desired Result:
To worship together.

hymnals
(Allow 5 minutes.)

S

CLOSING CONNECTION

PRAY A HYMN

Give each teen a hymnbook. Have the teens open to the hymn "Help Us Accept Each Other" (#560 in *The United Methodist Hymnal)* or a similar hymn if this hymn is not in your hymnal. Tell your group members to spend a moment or two silently reading the words of this hymn. Then invite your teens to offer this hymn as a circle prayer, each youth reading a phrase in turn until all of the verses have been read aloud.

Close with the following prayer:

> **God of all people, help us know in our hearts and in our actions that we are loved. Help us know in our hearts and in our actions that you love all people, even those who are very different from us. In Christ we pray, Amen.**

Read Me

THIS IS WHAT YOU NEED TO KNOW ABOUT THE TOPIC.

Preparing Yourself

Have you ever had a day when you felt unloved and unaccepted? At one time or another, most people have such a feeling. The teenagers in your class are very likely to have had such feelings. Adolescents particularly need to know of God's love for them. This unit provides opportunities for youth to understand themselves as created and loved by God. It also helps them to look beyond themselves to other people and to understand that God created and loves everyone—even those who are not like them. This session also provides opportunities for youth to identify and appreciate the diversity of human talents and skills.

Take a moment now to open your heart and mind to God's presence as you prepare to lead your group. Read Romans 9:20-25 and "Bible Background." What does the image of clay in this Scripture say to you?

Do the YouthPage for yourself. What insights did you gain from responding to the questions?

Think about each of the individuals in your group. Do any seem to need special affirmation of God's love? Who? How might you show that affirmation to him or her? Are any racial, ethnic, or nationality issues going on in the lives of the youth in your group? in your church? in the community where you live? How might those issues be discussed within the context of Romans 9:20-25? Are there socioeconomic issues that have caused division within your group, your church, or your community?

Pray for the youth with a prayer of your own or with the following prayer:

God of all people, thank you for making all of us in your image. Thank you for helping us to see that you love and value every individual on this planet. Help me to live your love. Help me reveal your love to the young people I seek to lead toward a richer and deeper faith in you. In Christ's name, Amen.

Bible Background

Paul's letter to the church at Rome is an account of Paul's belief. It is his theological statement, indeed, one of the very first theological statements developed by the early Christian church. In Romans Paul presents the essence of his understanding of the faith that would become known as Christianity.

Paul wrote the letter to prepare the church for his visit to Rome. His eyes were ever on the horizon, and he believed that Rome would make an excellent base of operations for his mission of spreading the gospel. Some suggest that Paul's ultimate aim was to proclaim the Gospel of Jesus Christ in Spain, recognized at that time as the farthest frontier of civilization.

The very first Christians were Jews. When Gentiles or non-Jews began to be baptized, some questions arose among the Jewish Christians and others about the identity of God's chosen people. In

Romans 9—11 Paul, who was a Jew and a Pharisee, argues that being a Jew is a matter of heart rather than a matter of birth. Anyone who has faith as Abraham had faith (Genesis 15:6) is chosen and will inherit the promises of God.

We are adopted as God's chosen people by virtue of God's mercy and love, Paul argues, rather than by virtue of our birth or a rigorous practice of a system of religious rules and regulations. It is not what we do, but rather what God does that saves us. We are called to trust in God's grace and to accept with love and gratitude what God has already done for us. Ethical choices emerge out of the response of gratitude: we live according to God's will, not out of fear of what God will do if we don't, but out of grateful response for what God has already done for us in Jesus Christ.

Paul's understanding is a shift from the notion of being born into God's salvation. Paul's explanation of Christ's grace and sacrifice also opens the door for all people to understand themselves as children of God. "There is no longer Jew or Greek, there is no longer slave or free, there is no longer male and female; for all of you are one in Christ Jesus" (Galatians 3 :28).

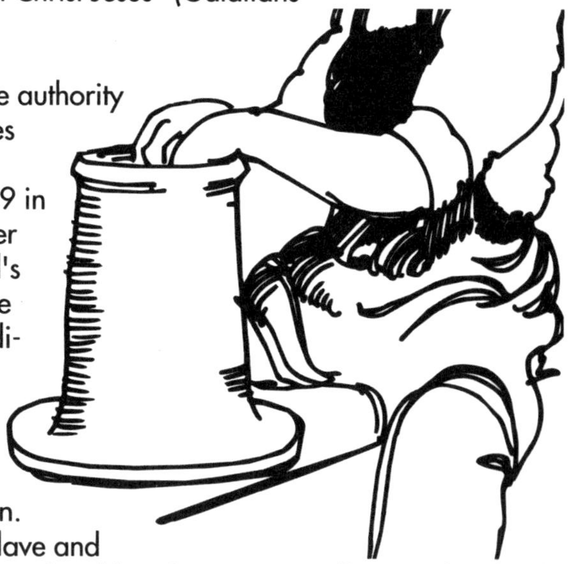

Romans 9:20-25 recognizes the authority of God as the Creator who loves and values all creation. Paul echoes Isaiah 29:16 and 45:8-9 in his use of the image of the potter and the clay to emphasize God's role. God creates from the same "clay" items for special and ordinary use. And yet, God makes no distinction between the "special" and the "ordinary." Both are loved totally, completely, and without qualification. All people, Jew and non-Jew, slave and free, rich and poor, male and female, old and young, are all created, valued, and loved by God.

Romans 9:25, which quotes the Old Testament prophet Hosea, summarizes God's inclusive love for all people. God's acceptance has nothing to do with a person's talents, parents, nationality, or accomplishments. In God's hands, in God's sight, and in God's heart all people are beloved and special.

THE SAME LUMP OF CLAY...

Has the potter no right over the clay, to make out of the same lump one object for special use and another for ordinary use?

(Romans 9:21)

What are some items made of pottery or china that are for special use?

What are some items made of pottery or china that are for ordinary use?

Do you think a special use is more important than an ordinary use? Why or why not?

What can you learn from Paul's image of the same lump of clay about people and their diverse talents?

Does God Love My Talents Or Me?

God loves both you and your talents, but God's love does not depend upon your talents. Talents are what we can do, not who we are.

Skills and talents are different for each of us. God has given each of us a set of skills, talents, abilities, and gifts that enable us to serve one another and serve God. Some people are fond of saying that they have no talents, that they can do nothing special. Because of God's grace, this is simply not true. God has given every one of us talents and gifts. Our failure to recognize what God has done for us, the gifts God has given us, reflects on our own misunderstanding of God and ourselves. An old but true expression says, "God made you, and God doesn't make junk!"

But—and this is important!—a person's identity does not depend upon the gifts and talents God has given that person. God loves us simply because God created us. God loves us, not because we perform this or that duty or exercise this or that talent. God's love is free and does not depend on what we do, or do not do.

Our best actions occur when we respond to God's love with gratitude, using whatever skills or talents we have to express our love for God and for our neighbors. And since we are all created and loved by God, we celebrate the skills and talents of other people.

SESSION 4:

TO OBEY AND TO SEE

FOCUS

To help youth examine a story from the life of Jesus and to discover the ways in which this story speaks directly to them.

SCRIPTURE

John 9:1-7

HERE'S THE PLAN | DO IT YOUR WAY

OPTIONS	TIME (minutes)	PREPARATION	SUPPLIES
INITIAL CONNECTION			
A "Would You?"	8	prepare three large signs labeled, "Would," "Wouldn't," and "Maybe, Maybe Not"	three large paper signs, open space for moving around
B Well, Did You?	8		moveable chairs or space to sit on the floor
CONNECT WITH THE SESSION			
A Whose Fault Is This?	8	prepare a "graffiti wall" by attaching a large sheet of paper on the wall	large sheet of paper such as butcher paper, colored markers
B Why Me, Lord?	8		movable chairs for a debate
CONNECT WITH THE BIBLE AND FAITH COMMUNITY			
A Hear a Bible Story	10		Bibles
B Roleplay a Bible Story	10	gather simple props for use in skits	Bibles, simple props for skits like sunglasses, small basin of water
CONNECT WITH LIFE			
A A Window on the World	8		large sheet of paper and markers, paper and pencils, Bibles
B Complete the Sentences	8		Bibles, paper and pencils or pens
CLOSING CONNECTION			
To See Clearly	8	make copies of YouthPage	Bibles, YouthPage

INITIAL CONNECTION

A "WOULD YOU?"

Before the session, make three large paper signs, one with the word "Would," a second with the word "Wouldn't" and a third with the words, "Maybe, Maybe Not." Tape or fasten one of these signs on each of three walls in your meeting space.

Tell the group members that you are going to read a series of statements. If a teen would do what is asked in the statement, she or he is to stand under the "Would" sign. If he or she would not do what the statement says, he or she should stand under the "Wouldn't" sign. If a teen is unsure, she or he should move to the "Maybe, Maybe Not" sign. Here are the statements:

- **Your parent tells you to clean up your room.**
- **A friend urges you to drive faster than the speed limit.**
- **Your youth group counselor asks you to skip a ball game and come to a youth group retreat.**
- **A teacher tells you to have your assignment in by Friday.**
- **Your best friend asks for a ten-dollar loan.**
- **Your pastor asks you to offer a prayer at the Sunday morning service.**
- **A small group of friends at school invite you to go skydiving with them.**
- **An elderly lady asks you to help her with her groceries.**
- **A stranger rubs some clay on your eyes, then tells you to go wash it off.**
- **A girl you barely know at school asks you to tell her about Jesus Christ.**

Read these statements quickly and ask the students to move to the signs quickly. You're looking for first impressions, not carefully considered answers. If only one or two youth gather at one sign in response to a statement, ask these youth why they chose as they did.

ASK:

- **Do others ever ask us to do things that seem unwise or don't make much sense?**

- **Does Jesus Christ ever ask us to do things that don't seem to make much sense? Explain.**

Desired Result:
To introduce the theme of obedience by getting youth to think about why they should or should not do what they are asked.
(Choose Option A or B.)

open space for moving around in the meeting area, three large paper signs
(Allow 8 minutes.)

moveable chairs or space to sit on the floor ***(Allow 8 minutes.)***

B WELL, DID YOU?

Divide the group into teams of three. Ask the youth in each team to pull their chairs together or to sit on the floor where they can talk together easily. Ask each team to discuss these questions. Be sure that each of the three members of each team has an opportunity to respond to every question:

ASK:

- **Has anyone ever asked you to do something you didn't want to do? Did you do it? Why? Describe this experience for your teammates.**
- **Has anyone ever asked you to do something you thought was really strange, unusual, or weird? Did you do it? Why? Describe the experience for your teammates.**
- **Has anyone ever asked you to do something really strange, something you didn't want to do, but you did it and were pleasantly surprised at the result? Describe the experience for your teammates. Why did you decide to do it even though you didn't want to do it at first?**

Hear brief reports from several of the teams.

Desired Result: To have youth begin thinking about why bad things happen and who is responsible for them. **(Choose Option A or B.)**

CONNECT WITH THE SESSION

large sheet of paper, colored markers ***(Allow 8 minutes.)***

A WHOSE FAULT IS THIS?

Fasten a large sheet of paper, perhaps a long strip of butcher paper, on a wall at a height where all members of your group can write on it. Write along the top edge of the sheet these words: "Whose Fault Is This?" Use this sheet as a "graffiti sheet." Share the following scenarios with your group members (putting each scenario into your own words and elaborating a bit, if you choose), then ask the youth to write on the graffiti sheet who they think is to blame in each scenario.

- **Three teenage brothers are arrested and imprisoned for possession of marijuana. Upon investigation, the police discover that the boys' parents are regular users of marijuana and other drugs. The parents grow marijuana in the family home. Who is to blame for the brothers' arrest and imprisonment?**
- **A teenage girl, whose parents are out of town for a weekend and left her home alone with permission to use the family car, runs a red light, collides with another car, and badly hurts the two occupants in the other car. Police discover that the girl had been drinking beer. She said she got the beer from a local convenience store and reported that the clerk**

at the convenience store did not ask her age or for identification. Who is to blame for the pain and suffering of the two occupants of the other car?

- **A young married couple want desperately to have a child. When they discover that they are expecting a baby, they both take several courses on childbirth and child-care. The mother-to-be watches her diet very carefully, gets the amount of exercise prescribed by her doctor, visits the doctor on a regular basis, seeks to reduce stress in her life, and does everything she can for her baby. The father-to-be is very supportive in every way. The child is born with serious physical problems and will need immediate and extensive surgery to try to repair the many problems. Who is to blame for the child's condition?**

After the youth have recorded their thoughts about the scenarios, look at the graffiti sheet as a group. What do you and the group see there? How often is the person most directly involved held responsible? How often are people other than the person directly involved viewed as responsible? How often do you see the words, "No one" or "God" or "Everyone" on the graffiti sheet? Talk as a whole group about who is to blame in each situation.

B WHY ME, LORD?

movable chairs for a debate
(Allow 8 minutes.)

ASK:

- **Do bad things ever happen to good people? Give some examples.**
- **Have bad things ever happened to you when you were trying to be good? Give some examples.**
- **Do bad people sometimes seem to "get ahead" and have things work their way? Give some examples.**
- **Have you ever done some bad things, yet things seemed to work out all right? Give some examples.**
- **Have you ever asked, "Why did this happen to me?" Describe such a time in your life.**

START HERE

Divide your group into two teams and stage a debate. Team 1 will argue that bad things happen only to bad people who deserve those bad things and that when bad things seem to happen to good people, it is because the people aren't really good. Team 2 will argue that bad things happen to good people and good things happen to bad people, and that's just the way it is; there's no explanation for it. Let the teams gather for a couple of minutes to select their spokespersons and to plan their arguments. Team 1 will have two minutes to present its argument, then Team 2 will have two minutes for its argument. Next, Team 1 will have one minute to reply to Team 2, and Team 2 will have one minute to reply to Team 1. Keep this light and fun, but do not let it become a shouting match!

Desired Result:
To examine the themes of obedience and responsibility in the story of the man born blind in John 9.
(Choose Activity A or B.)

Bibles
(Allow 10 minutes.)

CONNECT WITH THE BIBLE AND THE FAITH COMMUNITY

A HEAR A BIBLE STORY

In your own words tell the story of Jesus healing the man born blind in John 9:1-7. Feel free to put the story in a contemporary setting, if you choose, and to suggest thoughts and feelings that are not explicit in the biblical narrative. Be sure to emphasize three points in your story, for these three are the focal points of this session: 1) The question of responsibility for the man's condition: was it caused by the man's sin, by his parents' sin, or by something else? 2) In the hands of Jesus, clay or mud, a very common and ordinary element, effected healing and the restoration of sight; and 3) The man's faith and his willingness to do what Jesus asked him to do, even though it seemed simple and apparently useless, restored his sight.

After telling the story, ask your group members to reflect silently as you ask these questions:

ASK:

- **How do you think the parents of the man born blind felt when the disciples asked Jesus if the man had sinned or if his parents had sinned to cause him to be born without sight? Try to feel as the parents must have felt; try also to feel as the man himself must have felt.**
- **How do you think the man born blind felt when a stranger came up to him and rubbed clay on his sightless eyes? Put yourself in his shoes; how would you feel if such a thing happened to you?**
- **How do you think the man felt when the stranger told him to go and wash off the clay in a particular pool of water? Put your answers into words, phrases, or sentences the man may have thought, but perhaps did not dare say.**
- **Who or what do we try to blame for the problems and difficulties we may face?**
- **How has Jesus used simple things, like clay, to help you see something you had not been aware of?**
- **What is Jesus asking you to do that may seem strange or useless? What are some of the reasons we give for not doing what Jesus asks?**

B ROLEPLAY A BIBLE STORY

Bibles; simple props like sunglasses; a small basin of water
(Allow 10 minutes.)

Divide your group into two teams. Invite the members of both teams to read John 9:1-7 carefully. Now, make these assignments:

- Team 1 is to present the story of John 9:1-7 as a roleplay or skit.
- Team 2 is to present the story of John 9:1-7 as a pantomime or a skit without words.

Give the teams enough time to work out their presentations, assign parts, plan staging, and so on. Then ask each team to make its presentation.

ASK:

- **What differences did you experience between the spoken and the silent presentations? Which one seemed to tell the story the better?**
- **What new insights did you gain into the story by seeing it in pantomime? by listening to the dialogue the team had planned?**
- **Why do you think the disciples were so intent on assigning blame for the man's blindness?**
- **Why did Jesus make clay or mud to place on the man's eyes? Wouldn't Jesus' touch have been sufficient?**
- **How do you think the man felt when Jesus told him to go wash off the clay in a certain pool? Do you think the man had tried other cures for his blindness?**

CONNECT WITH LIFE

Desired Result:
To help teens begin to understand more how they are responsible for their own actions and the ways in which God calls them to obedient service.
(Choose Option A or B.)

A WINDOW ON THE WORLD

chalkboard and chalk or a large sheet of paper and colored markers; masking tape
(Allow 8 minutes.)

One of the major points of the story of Jesus and the man born blind is that we too need to see clearly. We need to see the ways in which we are, and at times are not, responsible for our own suffering; the ways in which we are called to obey Christ (and often do not); and the ways in which Jesus uses some of the most simple means to tell us what we need to know for a joyful life.

Invite one or two teens in your group to draw a large window on the chalkboard, several sheets of newsprint, or a large sheet of butcher paper. The teens can decorate the window anyway they choose, perhaps with a fancy window frame, curtains, a valence, and so on. Fasten the window to a wall at a height that everyone can reach.

Now distribute small pieces of paper, perhaps half-sheets of regular 8½ x 11 paper, to the members of the group. Ask each teen in your class to draw or sketch several things church people need to see more clearly. If the youth have trouble getting started, "prime the pump" with these suggestions:

- Twelve thousand children in the world die every hour of every day from hunger, malnutrition, and starvation.
- Suicide is a leading cause of death among teenagers.
- Inner city teenage boys run a very high risk of death or imprisonment before they reach the age of twenty-five.
- Numerous elderly people in our community are lonely, frightened, and alone.

Give the teens several minutes to draw their sketches; remind them that artistic quality does not count! Then ask them to tape or glue their sketches or pictures on the window they made. Let several youth describe their pictures and share the meaning of their sketches with the whole group.

ASK:

➤ **Why are church people often "blind" to the things you have drawn?**

➤ **Acting as a disciple of Jesus, what little things could you do to help the people of your church begin to see these things more clearly?**

➤ **How can church people begin to see and sense their own responsibility for the conditions that cause some of the things that you have all pictured?**

B COMPLETE THE SENTENCES

Bibles, paper, pencils or pens
(Allow 8 minutes.)

Give each group member a piece of paper and a pencil or pen. Invite the group to be in an attitude of prayer as you read several sentence stems. Ask each teen to complete each sentence for herself or himself, then to fold the paper and place it in her or his Bible where it can be referred to often.

➤ **One thing I need to see more clearly is...**

➤ **Jesus may be trying to touch me through...**

➤ **I will begin to take responsibility for...**

This is a private and personal exercise. Remind the group members that they are in an attitude of prayer as they listen, ponder their responses, and write. Do not allow sharing of sentence completions.

CLOSING CONNECTION

TO SEE CLEARLY

Invite each group member to read John 9:1-7 silently and to substitute his or her own name for "the man" and to correct the pronouns. Encourage each youth to put herself or himself in the middle of the story, hearing the disciples' question about her or his sinfulness, feeling Jesus touch her or his eyes with clay, sensing the cool water from the pool cleansing her or his eyes, then suddenly being able to see—clearly and honestly and lovingly!

Invite the teens to examine the YouthPage and to carry out during this week some of the suggestions it makes.

Ask the youth to stand in a circle and join hands. Ask each teen to pray silently that the person on his or her right and left might sense the presence of Jesus Christ, might begin to see clearly, and might know the joy of fellowship with Christ. Conclude the time of silence by praying for each group member by name, making your prayer as personal for each as possible.

Desired Result:
To ask God to help us see more clearly, more honestly, and more lovingly.
(Choose Activity A or B.)

Bibles, YouthPage
(Allow 8 minutes.)

Read Me

THIS IS WHAT YOU NEED TO KNOW ABOUT THE TOPIC.

PREPARING YOURSELF

"What does this have to do with clay?" Good question! Your question concerns how this session on Jesus healing the man born blind fits with the previous three sessions on the potter and the clay. "Yes, Jesus did use clay (mud in some translations) to anoint the man's eyes; but that is really stretching the point, right?"

In fact, this final session is a wind-up, not only to the unit on "The Potter and the Clay" but also to this entire quarter's sessions in CONNECT. It is a summary session that reexamines in many ways the journey of faith, the Holy Spirit, the choices each person must make, our need for Christ in our spiritual blindness, and the experiences of being shaped by God. So don't stretch too far to make this session fit in with the three on the potter and the clay. Just relax and go with it, mining the richness of this story from John's Gospel.

How do you prepare to get into a Bible story, especially a long narrative like the ninth chapter of John? A couple of suggestions: Pray for God's guidance and direction as you read and study. Read the chapter straight through quickly; don't worry about details. Get the sweep of the story. Now go back and reread the chapter carefully, thoughtfully, and above all, prayerfully. Make notes for yourself in order to keep the characters and sequence of actions straight. Use a Bible dictionary or a commentary to check out facts, places, and customs that you might not fully understand. For example, what was the prevailing attitude about sickness and disabilities at the time of Jesus? Was there anything special about the pool of Siloam? Why did the some of the Pharisees have such conflict with Jesus about this event?

Now reread the chapter for a third time (perhaps several more times). Each time, try to put yourself in the place of one of the characters: the man born blind, the man' parents, the questioning Pharisee, even Jesus. Try to imagine how the man must have felt when a stranger rubbed mud on his sightless eyes.

Next, pray some more. Ask God to disclose the truths of this story for you and for the youth in your class. Pray that the youth will be open to these truths, that they will discover their own spiritual blindness, that they will be willing to follow the simple commands of Jesus, and that they will understand that illness and disabilities are not punishments from God for the sins of others. Instead they may be opportunities to reflect God's glory. Close your prayer time by praying for each group member by name and situation. Pray especially for those who do not attend every Sunday, for those who seem reluctant to participate, for those who seem to need to entertain the others with jokes and horseplay, for those who do not seem to "fit in" as well as some others, for those who are seriously groping for truth. Pray for each of them—and for yourself—as you seek to grow in Christian faith and discipleship.

Bible BACKGROUND

John's Gospel is unique among the four New Testament Gospels. It was written considerably later than the other three and it bears the stamp of prayerful and careful reflective thinking on the part of its writer. While Mark is like the daily newspaper and Matthew and John are like weekly newsmagazines, John's book looks back on the event's of Christ's life, seeking to analyze and discover the meaning of the events. Some scholars have suggested, therefore, that the lengthy dialogues in John were probably not recorded verbatim but are reconstructions of what Jesus said.

The fascinating ninth chapter of John's Gospel is an example of just such a dialogue and situation. Note how it begins, as do so many of Jesus' teaching opportunities, with a question asked of Jesus by a disciple. In this case, the question contains within it the prevailing understanding of the time that illness and physical disability are the direct result of sin. The disciple merely wonders whose sin caused this man's blindness.

Jesus' answer must have taken the disciples aback. He immediately rejects the prevailing understanding of the relationship between sin and illness and instead points out that God can use even a situation such as this for God's glory.

The question is frequently asked: Why did Jesus make clay or mud, smear it on the man's sightless eyes, then direct him to go wash off the mud? After all, this argument goes, Jesus cured many others by a mere word or touch. But remember, in those cases, the person who was healed had asked for Christ's healing, and Christ responded that the person was healed by his or her own faith. Here the man born blind does not ask for healing. Is he a man of faith? How would Jesus know? Jesus gets his answer by asking the man to do a simple act, an act that the man would probably regard as senseless and useless. If the man had replied that Jesus' direction was useless, perhaps his blindness would not have been healed. But the fact that the man accepted Jesus' direction (even though he may not have understood it entirely) and carried it out to the best of his ability demonstrated and proved his faith. That faith was rewarded by new sight.

Much of the rest of this chapter concerns on-going conflicts with some of the Pharisees, those who were zealous about following the law and the commandments. Jesus had challenged them by turning their ways of looking at things upside down. But the man's restored sight demonstrates, once again, the power of God and the access each of us has to that power through our faith in Jesus Christ.

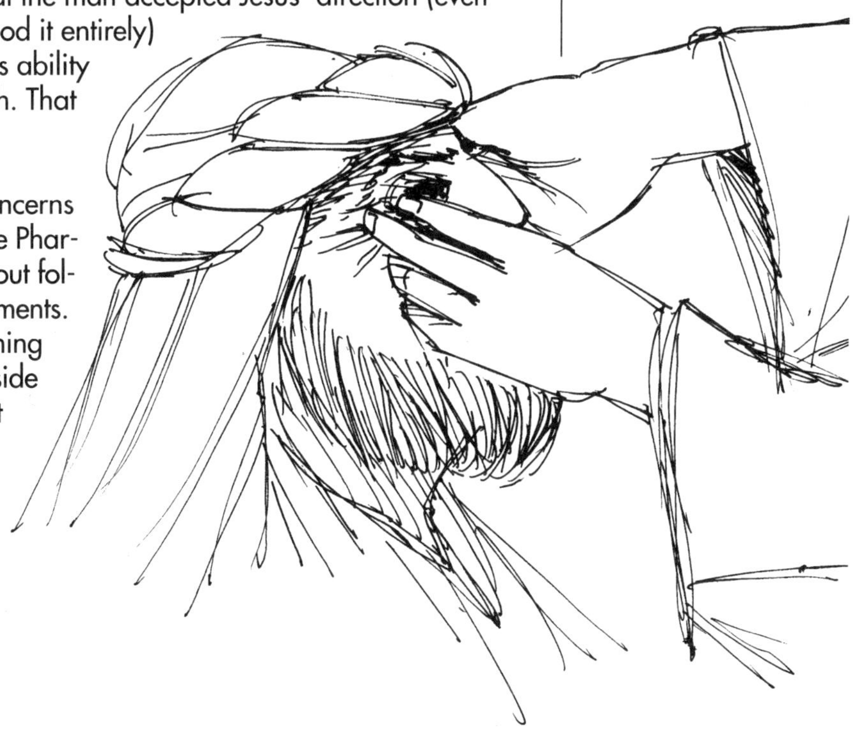

YOUTHPAGE

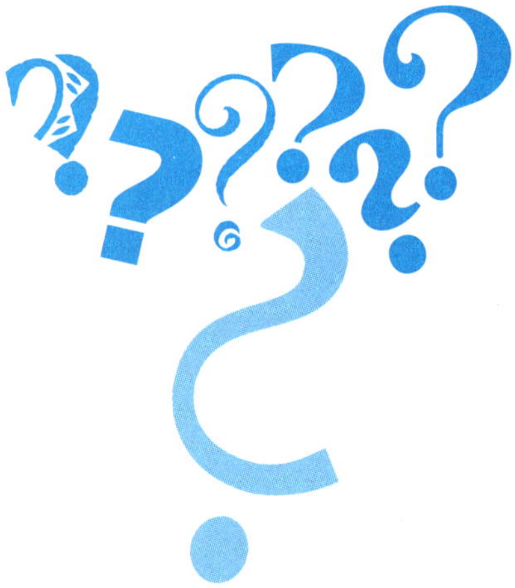

THE GIFT OF TRUE SIGHT

Jesus touched the eyes of a man who could not see with some simple clay and asked that man to wash off the clay. When the man did so, he could see!

During this week, think and pray about how you could help another person see— not in the physical sense, but "see" in the sense of understand or comprehend—how God loves that person, how that person might need to begin believing in God, how that person's life might be more fulfilled if he or she changed his or her actions. Use the journal page to keep track of your thoughts this week or jot them down here.

What can you do that will help that person see? Jot down some ideas here:

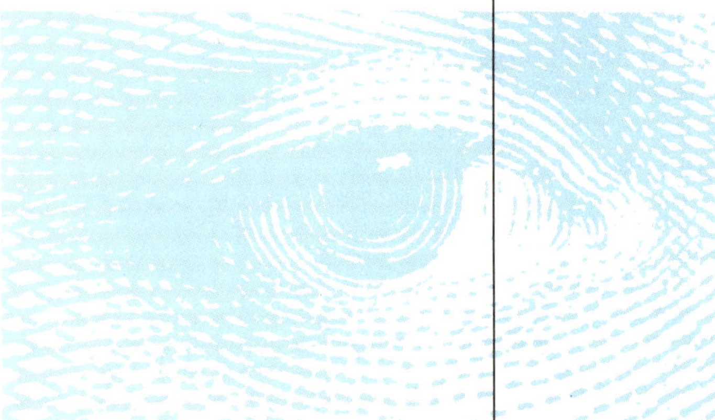

When you awaken each morning this week, ask God to guide your actions and to help you know what you should do today. Ask God to be as specific as possible. Remember, God may ask you to do great and mighty things or God may ask you to do something as simple as what Jesus asked of the man born blind. Listen intently for God's directions. Like Elijah, the answers may come in a still small voice; like Moses, the answers may come in something as dramatic as a burning bush; like John of Patmos, the answers may come in a dream or vision; like the Samaritan, the answers may come in tending to someone else's need; like Job, the answers may come from suffering and hardship.

YOUTHPAGE

Jot down here what you believe you have heard God calling to you to do. Do not share this page with anyone; this is between you and God.

Think long and hard, carefully and prayerfully, this week about the temptation you may have to blame your troubles on someone else. Sure, teachers can be unfair; friends can betray us; parents can be less than understanding; coaches can seem shortsighted; employers can be too demanding; life itself can seem unjust. But basically, some of the suffering each of us faces is of our own making, the result of our own self-centeredness and our own unwillingness to follow Jesus Christ.

Jot down here a list of the times during this week that you try to blame problems on someone else when the problems are indeed of your own making. This is not say that all of your problems are of your own making; it takes discernment and prayer to tell the difference. So before you write anything here, ask God to help you recognize what part you play, if any, in the problems you face.

If you are not already doing so, start each day this week with a prayer, spoken or silent. Offer a prayer to God each noontime, silently or aloud. Pray to God as you go to bed each evening, aloud or within your heart, trusting that God hears both.

Hey! Copy this page for your youth—really, we want you to!

Journal

DATE ______________________

DATE ______________________